One Bowl

Simple Healthy Recipes for One

Stephanie Bostic

Photography by Emily Kuross Vikre

Printed by CreateSpace

My sincerest thanks to all those who read, tasted, washed dishes, photographed, supported, corrected, and encouraged me along the way. Particular thanks to Catherine Fredman, for being my college mentor; Emily Kuross Vikre, for her food photography; Margaret Birnbaum for cover design; and to both my mother and Ellen Goldstein, for their careful editing.

Photography: **Emily Kuross Vikre**

Cover Design: **Margaret Birmbaum**

ISBN: 978-1-463-69072-4

Printed by CreateSpace

One Bowl

by

Stephanie Bostic

Table of Contents

Introduction

It's oddly difficult to cook for one. I've struggled with the experience: finding myself thinking it's too hard or takes too long to cook for one, eating cereal for supper, and spending more time washing dishes than eating! *One Bowl* emerged from my quest to solve those problems while eating tasty, healthy real food. I may occasionally still rely on takeout, but the following recipes make it easy to throw together a meal faster than a pizza would arrive. The next few chapters are your guidebook to reexamining your pantry, shopping skills, and food prep techniques to better feed yourself and fuel your life. Whether you are 20 and living in a dorm or 80 and living alone, you'll find the information, recipes, and suggestions you need to help you eat well.

One Bowl: Simple Healthy Recipes for One walks you through

- ➢ Eating more fruits and vegetables
- ➢ Eating less packaged food
- ➢ Quick healthy meals for one
- ➢ Recipes designed for one
- ➢ Enjoying new flavors

The first section, "Your Kitchen," will help you look at your equipment and healthy ways to stock your kitchen. With a stocked kitchen, throwing together a quick meal without going to the store or for takeout is straightforward and fast. It is possible to make a healthful delicious meal with food from the freezer and a can, but only if the freezer and pantry contain healthy ingredients.

The middle section contains the fun part—recipes! From breakfast through dessert, you'll find delicious recipes sized for one (with a few exceptions). You may find the sizes, designed for an average appetite, generous or small. Feel free to adjust the quantities, or to save the leftovers for another snack or meal. Novices will find basic guidance for how to adapt recipes within many of the recipes here. Not having a particular ingredient shouldn't stop you from making the recipe. The **Technique** listings explain basics such as how to cook an egg, use herbs, or store food safely. The glossary, at the end of the book, explains common cooking terms to help you decipher, for example, the difference between a simmer and a boil.

Most recipes focus on whole plant-based ingredients, for their budget, health, and environmental benefits. (Industrial livestock production can be very detrimental to the soil, water, air, and workers'/neighbors' health.) Many of my recipes were developed when I was in college or grad school, and on a strict budget, so beans and lentils were an affordable source of protein. As it happens, they are also one of the most nutrient-dense sources of protein available. You'll find beans and lentils featured in sandwich spreads, pasta dishes, soups, and salads. The meat and fish section offers a few quick favorites for the times when you can source sustainable meat and fish.

While breakfast has its own section, feel free to try sandwiches (perhaps the Lemon Artichoke Spread, or Black Olive Tuna Salad?), soups, or even desserts at breakfast. Breakfast dishes like Creamy Buckwheat with Berries or Southwest Frittata work for a quick lunch or supper too!

For the last section, "Nutrition Basics", I've used my background in human nutrition and research to write a brief, user-friendly overview. You'll also find a few quizzes and worksheets to help you examine your eating habits and plan ways to incorporate more fruits and vegetables into your diet. Please discuss specific concerns and changes with your health care provider in relation to your personal health.

Your Kitchen

A kitchen can be 8 feet by 4 feet, or it can be larger than most master bedrooms. You will need access to a very few basics: two burners, a refrigerator, a freezer, and preferably a microwave. You can live without the freezer, but it makes life easier. An oven, broiler, and toaster are also useful, but not as necessary. Two to six square feet of counter space or a table are also necessary. While you can balance a cutting board on top of a milk crate in a dorm room, the table is much more stable (and therefore much safer).

Stocking your pantry will make it easy to throw together a last minute meal, or skip grocery shopping one week when you find yourself overwhelmed with other things. View my list as a starting point and adapt it to your space, tastes, dietary restrictions, and budget.

Equipment

Cooking is easier with good tools. Look for solid materials that will wear well, and consider them an investment worth caring for. Midrange brands such as Cuisinart, Revere, or Farberware tend to provide lifetime service and are reasonably priced. If you're on a budget, try finding pieces on sale, at garage or moving sales, or in second hand stores.

Equipment Features

Pots: Look for heavy bottoms, such as stainless steel–coated copper.

Knives: Look for comfort in your hand and sharpness.

Mixing bowls: Glass can go in the microwave, but stainless steel are also durable.

Baking dishes: Look for something oven and microwave safe.

The Absolutely Essential box lists the minimum. From there, you can upgrade to additional useful items as needed. Keep in mind what you are likely to make—for example, a rice cooker might be more useful if you eat rice often, while a non-stick griddle could be useful if you enjoy pancakes every weekend.

Absolutely Essential:

8" or 10" chef's knife

Cutting board, 8" by 11"

Plastic cutting board (for meat and poultry)

Large wooden spoon

Measuring cups & spoons

Sauté pan, 8" or 10", with lid

Storage containers or jars

Spatula, for flipping items

Manual can opener

Fire extinguisher

 2-quart pot & lid

Very useful:

3-quart pot & lid

Mixing bowls, 3 sizes

1 quart baking dish

8" square pan or deep pie pan

Cheese grater or microplane

Coffeepot or teapot

Vegetable peeler

 Paring knife

Colander

Quite convenient:

Blender or food processor

Whisk

Slotted spoon

Cookie sheet

Small frying pan, 6"

Pasta or stock pot

Limited storage space definitely affects your options. Try substituting a collapsing colander, an immersion blender, and make sure your bowls, pots, and pans nest within each other.

Pantry

Your pantry should reflect what you like to eat (within reason!). If you don't like rice, buy bulgur or quinoa or polenta instead. The items in Probably Useful are those that are nice to have on hand, but if you're short on space, buy it only when you're planning to use it.

Cans & Jars
Beans, low sodium
Olive oil
Canola or peanut oil
White wine vinegar
Mustard

Dried:
Pasta
Lentils and dried beans
Brown rice
Oatmeal or buckwheat
Baking powder
Herbs and spices

Frozen:
Vegetables
Fruit

Perishables:
Milk or fortified soy milk
Bread, tortillas, or crackers
Cheese
Eggs
Butter
Onions or shallots
Garlic
Potatoes or sweet potatoes
Seasonal fruits and vegetables

Probably useful:
Marinated artichokes
Balsamic vinegar
Sugar
Flour
Tuna or salmon, canned
Tomato sauce and paste
Nuts and seeds
Dried fruit
Natural peanut butter
Salsa
Soy sauce
Chili sauce

Eating seasonally means that you buy items that are ripe in your region at that time. In New England, I eat asparagus in the late spring and pumpkins in the autumn. Eating seasonally helps ensure you are eating a variety of foods throughout the year, means your food is fresher, and produce is often less expensive in season.

5

Meal Planning

One of the benefits of cooking only for yourself is that you can be very flexible. Stocking your pantry is only helpful if your pantry yields the food you want to cook and eat, so focus on foods you like.

Planning out your meals beforehand can help you judge how much food to buy as well as making cooking for the week (or month) easier. Thinking beforehand helps you save time later! As you plan, consider:

- Sales or coupons
- Time for shopping and cooking
- Seasonal foods
- Packed lunches/meals
- Variety

Select a few main foods to plan around, and find recipes for each. Once you have your recipes, look at ingredients. Check your pantry, and make your shopping lists for the grocery store, meat or fish market, and/or farmer's market. Don't forget to add any extra items not in recipes like dish soap, fruit, snacks, coffee, or bread for sandwiches.

Don't like meal planning? Keep your pantry staples well-stocked, and be careful to not go overboard on perishable items. Set aside time twice a week to review your supplies and eat anything that could spoil soon.

Expanding Horizons

Trying small amounts of new or disliked foods is actually sensible. You may have a failure (I, for example, just don't like okra) but you may discover that something you hated boiled or canned is pretty good when it's steamed with peanut sauce. Be sure to prepare it in a new way!

Recipes

From breakfast to dessert, you'll find ideas and instructions for basic combinations that are both delicious and healthy. I've tried to keep ingredient lists on the shorter side, and have avoided using special equipment to make them easy. Feel free to adapt them to your tastes—you may not like cumin as much as I do, or perhaps you adore tomatoes and want four where I would use just a tablespoon or two. One of the best parts of cooking for one is that you can cook entirely for yourself.

Given the ideal of eating half fruits and vegetables, most of the recipes have substantial amounts of either vegetables or fruits. You can substitute similar vegetables—like using cauliflower instead of broccoli, or turnips instead of carrots—if that's what you have in the pantry. With the exception of baked goods, everything else should have some flexibility (adapt cooking times when necessary). Enjoy!

Reading Recipes

Times: The times listed assume you are familiar with the recipe and comfortable in the kitchen. Recipes are sorted from least to most time-consuming.

Servings: The number of servings you will get from a recipe depends on your appetite. Most of these recipes serve one generously, with a few exceptions for items that store or freeze particularly well.

Temperatures: Some stoves have low settings that are actually warm settings, and high settings vary similarly. I recommend watching your stove closely until you are accustomed to which settings are close to what I suggest.

Ingredients: I've listed ingredients in US measures or by a description. When an item is described (i.e. 1 small apple), the recipe is flexible. Metric conversions are readily available through Google or other online calculators.

Abbreviations of US measurements:

Pound	lb
Ounce	oz
Cup	c
Tablespoon	T
Teaspoon	t

Conversions:

3 t = 1 T

8 T = 1 c

8 fluid oz = 1 c

16 oz = 1 lb

Adapting to restricted diets

Most of the recipes are vegetarian, and many can easily be converted to vegan, egg-free, nut-free, soy-free, or dairy-free by leaving out those ingredients or using substitutes. However, limited testing has been done utilizing those substitutions. All recipes have been tested using wheat and gluten-free substitutes. Contact the author at http://onebowlcookbook.com for more details.

Breakfast

Breakfast is an excellent opportunity to add more fruits and vegetables to your diet, or to enjoy a bowl full of whole grains. Try adding fresh cranberries and toasted almonds to dress up a basic hot cereal. Toss some vegetables into your morning eggs, and you are off to a great start. Many later recipes are equally appropriate for breakfast. Sweet Potato and Black Bean Soup with Lime (Soups and Salads) would hold you through a long morning, while Rice Pudding (Desserts) would also stick to your ribs. Explore your options!

Technique: Cooking Eggs

Breakfast Parfait

Spiced Oatmeal with Apple

Creamy Buckwheat with Berries

Eggs with Greens

Poached Eggs Florentine

Southwest Frittata

Apple Pancakes

Vegetable Bread Pudding

Individual Spinach Frittatas

Corn Muffins

Technique: Cooking Eggs

Eggs come in a perfect serving size, and pack a nice punch of protein for not too many calories. I eat them regularly for a quick supper, breakfast, or late lunch.

Hard-boiled: Place the eggs in a pot over medium heat with just enough cold water to cover them. Set a timer for 20 minutes. When the water comes to a boil, turn down to a simmer immediately to prevent the eggs from cracking open. Remove from the heat and drain after the timer goes off. Rinse in cold water several times if they are going to be eaten cold.

Fried: Over low heat, melt butter (or heat oil) in a small skillet. Meanwhile, crack each egg into a small bowl or custard cup. When the pan is hot enough to sizzle when you drip a little water on it carefully add the egg(s). Cook until the egg is firm, spooning extra butter or oil over the egg before removing from the pan. You can also flip your egg, if you prefer.

Omelet: Beat egg(s) with 1 T milk in a bowl. Heat 1 T butter or oil in an omelet pan or small skillet over medium heat. When hot, swirl to coat the pan with the butter. Add the eggs. After 1-2 minutes, place 2-3 T filling on half the egg. Loosen the edges with a spatula. Carefully slide a spatula under the other half of the egg and flip it over the filling. Reduce heat, and cook for another minute.

Eggs commonly carry *Salmonella,* a bacteria that leads to food poisoning. To help prevent illness:

- cook eggs to 160°F
- store in the refrigerator
- use pasteurized eggs in recipes requiring raw egg
- keep hot dishes hot and cold dishes cold
- wash hands after handling eggs.

Poached: Fill a shallow saucepan or deep skillet with 2-3" of water. Add 1 t vinegar. Bring to a simmer. Crack an egg into a small bowl or measuring cup. Carefully pour into the simmering water. Simmer the egg for 3 minutes and remove with a slotted spoon.

Scrambled: Beat an egg in a bowl with 1 T milk or water. Heat 1 T butter or olive oil in a small skillet (add more to coat the bottom if using a larger skillet). When the pan is hot, swirl the butter to coat the bottom and pour in the egg. Top with salt, pepper, or any other seasoning. Stir slowly, from the outside to the middle, until done to your taste.

Satisfying meals are made from a balance of textures, nutrients, flavors, and food groups.

☐ food groups: protein, grain, dairy, fruit, vegetable

☐ filling nutrients: water, fiber, fat

☐ flavors: sweet, sour, bitter, salty, umami (savory)

☐ textures: crunchy, creamy, soft, chewy, tender

One rule of thumb is to aim for foods from three or more food groups at each meal. Typically, that also gives you several flavors and often a couple of textures as well. Three seems to be a minimum, but the most brilliant meals often include all five flavors and most textures. As an added benefit, you'll often manage to eat a nice range of nutrients too.

Simply adding a few raisins for sweetness, lemon juice for sourness, mushrooms for a savory flavor, and olive oil for fat can make sautéed collard greens exciting and a substantial, nutritious meal. Balancing and aligning all the puzzle pieces coalesces "food" into a "meal."

Breakfast Parfait

5 minutes

In the US, parfaits were originally ice cream and fruit desserts. Substituting yogurt for the ice cream and adding some toast yields a basic breakfast. Commercially packaged yogurt with fruit or granola tends be very sweet—throwing together your own is both healthier and often less expensive. Flavorful sweeteners such as brown sugar or real maple syrup help make yogurt seem sweeter than it actually is. Try using whole grain toast for the healthiest option.

1 c fruit pieces (bananas, berries, peaches, etc.)

$^2/_3$ c plain or unsweetened vanilla yogurt

2 thin slices toast, cut into triangles

1 t brown sugar or 100% real maple syrup

Spoon the yogurt into a bowl, top with the fruit and place toast triangles around the outside of the bowl. Sprinkle with sugar or syrup.

Variation: Use rice cakes or whole grain crackers instead of toast.

American breakfasts tend to be high in sugar, high in fat, or high in both sugar and fat. A simple rule of thumb is to try to aim for less than 2 teaspoons (8 g) added sweetener such as sugar, brown sugar, maple syrup, corn syrup, malt, evaporated cane juice, molasses, or anything that ends with "-ose." If you read the ingredients labels, you'll be able to spot added sugars. Naturally occurring sugars, like those found in apples or raisins, are an exception.

Spiced Oatmeal with Apple

10 minutes

Oatmeal is both a great comfort food and an excellent whole grain breakfast. Mixed with spices and fruit, it makes a healthy but still sweet breakfast. If you have extra time, try making steel cut oats instead of rolled oats.

$\frac{1}{3}$ **c oatmeal, quick or old fashioned**

$\frac{2}{3}$ **c water or milk**

2 T nuts, chopped

2 T raisins, dried apricot pieces, or date pieces

1 small apple, cored and chopped

$\frac{1}{8}$ **t cinnamon or dried ginger**

Pinch cloves

Milk to taste

Mix the spices, oatmeal, water or milk, nuts, and raw apple in a large bowl if cooking in the microwave, or in a saucepan if cooking on the stove. Cook oatmeal according to the oatmeal package until done, stirring frequently. Add the raisins, and additional milk if desired.

Variation: Substitute a sliced banana, pear, or peach for the apple.

Creamy Buckwheat with Berries

10 minutes

Cream of buckwheat makes a nice change from oatmeal if you like hot cereal. It cooks quickly, and is readily available in the natural foods aisle or (sometimes) with the baby food.

3 T dry cream of buckwheat cereal

$\frac{1}{4}$ t ground cinnamon

$\frac{1}{3}$ c frozen cranberries (fresh, in season)

$\frac{1}{3}$ c frozen blueberries (fresh, in season)

1 t ground flaxseed

3 T sliced almonds

1-2 t maple syrup

Optional: 3-4 T milk

Place the buckwheat cereal in a bowl with 3/4 c water. Soak overnight (or just while you make your coffee). Microwave, or cook on the stovetop, for 2-10 minutes. If you soaked it overnight, it will need less time. Add the cinnamon, berries, flaxseed, almonds, and maple syrup and heat for another 1-2 minutes or until the berries have warmed. Top with milk, if desired.

Variation: Use diced fruit such as peaches or plums instead of berries.

Eggs with Greens

10 minutes

Savory breakfasts can be a great way to incorporate more vegetables into your day. Served over rice, or with an English muffin, this will start your day with a nice blend of protein, vitamins, minerals, and carbohydrates.

2 eggs

2 T milk or water

2 c spinach, kale, bok choi, chard, or other greens

1 clove garlic, minced

1 T olive oil

Wash and chop the greens coarsely. Heat the oil in a small skillet over medium heat. Meanwhile, beat the eggs with the milk. When the skillet is hot, add the garlic, stir briefly, and stir in the greens. Cook until wilted and tender, then pour in the eggs. Cook until firm, stirring for scrambled eggs or covering with a lid for a frittata.

Variation: Add 1 t dried or fresh herbs such as oregano or chives. Or, add a few drops of soy sauce and serve with chili garlic sauce.

Where's the bacon?

Processed meats such as bacon, ham, deli-style lunchmeats, and sausage have very high levels of salt and saturated fat. They have also been linked to greater risk of heart disease, diabetes, and cancer. For that reason, I recommend avoiding them for regular meals and eating eggs, fruit, nuts or cereals for everyday breakfasts.

Some people enjoy eating fresh meats (homemade sausage from freshly ground turkey is one example) instead or consuming them very rarely, on special occasions or when eating out.

Poached Eggs Florentine

15 minutes

Florentine dishes always involve spinach. Catherine de Medici popularized spinach in the French courts, and so dishes with spinach were named Florentine in honor of her city of origin, Florence.

1 t white or cider vinegar

2 eggs

4 oz fresh or frozen spinach

1 English muffin

1 T butter, melted

1 T Parmesan or Asiago cheese, grated

Pepper to taste

Grease a wide shallow saucepan or deep skillet. Fill with the vinegar and 2" water. Place over medium heat. Crack each egg into a measuring cup or custard dish. Meanwhile, wash the spinach well but do not dry. Wilt the spinach in a covered bowl or casserole by microwaving for 30 to 90 seconds. Drain and add half the butter to the spinach.

When the water in the skillet is simmering, carefully pour the eggs into the pan, as far apart as possible. Do not allow the eggs to touch. Keep the water at a gentle simmer. Occasionally spoon hot water over the eggs. While the eggs cook, toast and butter the English muffin lightly. Top with the spinach.

After 3 minutes, use a slotted spoon to remove the eggs and place them on the spinach. Top with cheese and pepper, if desired, and enjoy.

Southwest Frittata

15 minutes

Even if you don't normally eat two eggs, make the full recipe. The leftovers are great cold wrapped in a tortilla for lunch or a snack.

2 T oil

$\frac{1}{2}$ onion, diced

$\frac{1}{3}$ c diced red or yellow pepper

2 eggs

2 T milk or water

Pinch chili powder

$\frac{1}{3}$ c frozen or fresh corn

6 black olives

1 generous handful baby spinach or 3 leaves chard, chopped

Salsa, to taste

Cilantro, to taste

Optional: 3 T grated cheese

> **Note:** If your skillet is not oven proof, transfer the cooked vegetables to a small greased casserole dish, pour the egg mixture over them, top with cheese, and bake at 425°F for 20 minutes.

In a small oven-proof skillet, heat the oil and add the onion and pepper. Cook over medium high heat, stirring occasionally. Meanwhile, beat the eggs with the milk. When the onions are translucent, add the chili powder, corn, greens, and olives. Stir until the greens are wilted and the corn has thawed. Turn on the broiler.

Pour the eggs over the vegetables, turn the burner heat to low, and cook for 5 minutes. Top the eggs with the cilantro, salsa, and cheese (if used). Broil for another 5 minutes or until a knife inserted into the center comes out clean.

Apple Pancakes

15 minutes

Pancakes are surprisingly fast when you only cook one batch. Banana or berries also work, but I enjoy apple the most!

$\frac{1}{2}$ c diced apple

3 T whole wheat flour

3 T white flour

$\frac{1}{2}$ t baking powder

$\frac{1}{8}$ t baking soda

2 t sugar or maple syrup

2 T beaten egg (about $\frac{1}{2}$ an egg)

$\frac{1}{4}$ t cinnamon

$\frac{1}{2}$ c buttermilk

1 T oil or melted butter, plus enough to grease the pan

Optional: 2 T chopped walnuts

> Store extra egg in the fridge to cook the next day in scrambled eggs or bread pudding. Alternatively, freeze it for the next batch of pancakes.

Thoroughly mix the flours, baking powder, baking soda, and cinnamon in a small bowl. Beat the buttermilk, egg, sugar, and oil together in another bowl. Heat a griddle or frying pan and coat with oil or butter. Add the apple to the liquid ingredients. Mix the wet ingredients into the dry ingredients. Stir until combined. Pour $\frac{1}{3}$ c batter onto the griddle when warm and cook until lightly browned on each side. Up to four pancakes may be cooked at once, depending on the size of your pan. Serve with fruit, or nut butter.

Variation: Use grated carrot instead of apple.

18

Vegetable Bread Pudding

30 minutes

Combining protein, grains, vegetables, and dairy, savory bread puddings work not only for breakfast but also for lunch or dinner.

1 small zucchini or yellow squash, grated (about ¾ c)

1 t salt

1 Roma tomato, chopped and seeded

1 slice stale bread, ideally bakery bread, torn into small pieces

2 eggs

2 T chopped fresh parsley or basil

¼ c yogurt, buttermilk, or evaporated milk

¼ c grated mozzarella or cheddar cheese

Black pepper to taste

Butter or spray to grease the pan

Optional: 2 T Parmesan

Lightly salt the zucchini and place it in a colander, allowing it to drain. Let it drain for 10–15 minutes while you prepare the other items.

Preheat the oven to 350°F. Grease a small casserole (1 quart) dish. Mix the tomato, bread, eggs, yogurt, cheese (if using), and herbs in a bowl. Rinse the zucchini and press with your hands to remove water. Stir into the egg mix. Pour into the pan and bake for 15–20 minutes or until firm to the touch.

Individual Spinach Frittatas

40 minutes

Muffins tins make a perfectly sized frittata—just right for a light breakfast. Not only that, they freeze well. Make a batch on the weekend, and you have breakfast and snacks all week. No spinach in the house? Substitute leftover steamed broccoli, cauliflower, kale, collards, or sautéed onions.

8 eggs

2 c frozen spinach, defrosted or cooked fresh spinach

$^2/_3$ c milk or plain yogurt

8 oz sharp cheddar, grated

4 oz Parmesan, grated

1 medium sweet potato

Butter or spray for greasing the pan

Optional: **$^1/_8$ t chili flakes or chili sauce**

  $^1/_4$ t thyme

  $^1/_4$ t dried oregano

Pierce the sweet potato several times with a fork and bake in the microwave until tender. Remove and cool. Meanwhile, preheat oven to 400°F. Grease muffin tins. Beat together the eggs, milk, chili, and herbs. Peel, quarter, and slice the sweet potato. Layer the sweet potato, spinach, and cheeses in each cup, ending with a cheese layer on top. Pour the egg and milk mixture over the vegetables. Bake for 20 minutes or until golden brown on top.

Variation: Substitute tuna for Parmesan.

Corn Muffins

40 minutes

Soaking part of the cornmeal and using a little apple helps keep these muffins moist and cuts down on the sugar and oil. Most cornmeal is refined (the germ and bran removed), but you can find whole grain cornmeal at some stores. Store it in the freezer, unless you will use it within 3 months.

$\frac{1}{2}$ c + $\frac{1}{3}$ c fine cornmeal

1 c milk

$\frac{1}{3}$ c corn flour

$\frac{1}{3}$ c all purpose flour

1 T baking powder

2 T sugar

2 large eggs

4 T oil

$\frac{1}{2}$ c grated apple

Butter or cooking spray for greasing the pan

Place $\frac{1}{2}$ c cornmeal in a small mixing bowl with the milk. Stir well and let soak. Grease muffin tins well. Preheat oven to 375°F. Mix $\frac{1}{3}$ c cornmeal, corn flour, flour, baking powder, and sugar in a medium-sized mixing bowl. Add the eggs, oil, and grated apple to the milk mixture. Mix wet ingredients into the dry ingredients lightly and quickly until just blended. Spoon into muffin tins and bake for 20 minutes.

Variation: Use yellow squash instead of the apple.

Sauces and Dressings

Basic sauces and dressings can turn a plain meal into something more interesting with relatively little effort. Almost anything tastes better tossed with a little vinaigrette, and even bland leftovers shine under a garlic-basil dressing. Peanut sauce, in particular, is handy to have in the fridge for a quick meal.

Making your own salad dressing helps reduce added salt and sugar content, while also being fresher and less expensive. Start with these basic recipes, and then develop variations to *your* taste!

Technique: Using Herbs & Spices

Basic Vinaigrette

White Sauce

Peanut Sauce

Garlic Herb Pizza Sauce

Technique: Using Herbs & Spices

Herbs and spices are key to adding variety and flavor to recipes. The chart below suggests both seasoning combos and foods that work well together.

Herb	Foods	Combinations
Basil	Broccoli, fresh cheeses, pastas, poultry, salads, tomatoes	Basil, oregano, garlic, & lemon Basil, mint, & cilantro
Bay	Fish, lentils, pork, soups	Bay, rosemary, & thyme Bay, mustard seeds, & cumin
Chives	Eggs, fish, fresh cheeses, potatoes, vegetables	Chives & sour cream
Cilantro	Avocado, black beans, chili, meats, tomato	Basil, mint & cilantro Green chilies, lime, onion, & cilantro
Dill	Beans, cauliflower, cucumber, fish, potatoes	Prepared mustard & dill Sour cream, garlic, & dill
Marjoram	Eggs, lemon, poultry, vegetables, white beans	Marjoram, thyme, & sage Marjoram, garlic, & onion
Mint	Cucumber, lamb, peas, rice	Basil, mint, & cilantro Yogurt, garlic, & mint
Oregano	Beans, eggplant, meats, summer squash, tomato	Oregano, lemon, garlic, & olive oil Chili powder, cumin, & oregano
Parsley	Celery, grains, potatoes, tomatoes	Parsley, butter, & garlic
Rosemary	Meat, potatoes, zucchini	Garlic, rosemary, & olive oil
Sage	Butternut squash, poultry, sausage, white beans	Sage, thyme, & garlic Sage, nutmeg, & cream
Tarragon	Beans, potatoes, poultry	Tarragon & lemon
Thyme	Fish, lentils, meat, potatoes, soup	Thyme, sage, & garlic Thyme, onion, garlic, & lemon

Spice	Foods	Combinations
Allspice	Fruits, meats, sausage	Allspice, cinnamon, & nutmeg
Cinnamon	Carrots, fruits, grains, meat, sweet potatoes	Honey, cinnamon, & ginger Cinnamon, cloves, allspice, & ginger
Chili Powder	Beans, meats, onions	Chili powder, cumin, garlic, & onions Chili powder, lime, & onion
Chili Peppers	Beans, meats, pasta, vegetables	Chili, cumin, ginger, mustard, & turmeric Chili, garlic, oregano, & olive oil
Cloves	Fruits, meats, sweet potatoes	Cinnamon, cloves, allspice, & nutmeg
Cumin	Beans, meats, vegetables	Chili, cumin, garlic, & onion Chili, cumin, ginger, mustard, & turmeric
Garlic	Eggs, beans, meat, pasta, poultry, vegetables	Chili, garlic, oregano, & olive oil Thyme, onion, garlic, & lemon
Ginger	Coconut milk, meat, rice, tofu, vegetables	Ginger, garlic, oregano, & vermouth Ginger, soy sauce, garlic, & lime
Turmeric	Potatoes, lentils, rice	Chili, cumin, mustard, & turmeric

Herbs & Spices Quick Tips

➢ *Store them in cool, dark places.*
➢ *1 teaspoon dried = 1 Tablespoon fresh.*
➢ *Replace after 1 year.*
➢ *Toasting spices or dried herbs in oil or simmering them intensifies flavors.*
➢ *Add fresh herbs at the end of cooking.*

Basic Vinaigrette

5 minutes

Fresh salad dressing is a great improvement over the bottled type, and you can often use higher quality ingredients than found in bottled dressings. It is also an affordable way to explore the use of herbs and spices.

Vinaigrettes are an easy way to dress up leftovers as well as greens. Toss with leftover steamed vegetables, cooked grains like rice or quinoa, canned or leftover beans, or even tuna or chicken for more substantial salads.

1 t vinegar (balsamic, white wine, or red wine)

2 t olive oil

$\frac{1}{4}$ t Dijon mustard

$\frac{1}{4}$ t dried thyme, oregano, or basil

Optional: $\frac{1}{4}$ small clove garlic, minced

Mix ingredients in the jar. Cover tightly with the lid. Shake until well mixed. Store in the refrigerator. If you are dressing dry salad greens (as opposed to recently washed ones), or pre-cooked rice, add a few drops of water to the dressing.

Variations: Add 4–5 fresh minced basil leaves, 1 t lemon juice, and 2 t finely grated parmesan to make Basil Garlic Vinaigrette. Alternatively, add a few drops of honey for a light Honey Mustard Dressing.

White Sauce

10-15 minutes

White sauce is one base of European cuisine. This is a very basic version, but you can dress it up by adding flavors such as mushrooms, mustard, tarragon, wine, curry powder, cheese, or simply diced onion. The ratios below create a thin white sauce—perfect for cream soups or to drizzle over something a little too dry. Double the flour and butter to make a thicker white sauce, appropriate for casserole bases, or a more substantial sauce.

$\frac{1}{2}$ **c milk, cold**

1$\frac{1}{2}$ t butter

1$\frac{1}{2}$ t flour

Melt the butter in a small saucepan over medium low heat. Add the flour and stir until it is lightly toasted—about 1–2 minutes. Whisk in all the cold milk quickly, and stir for 2-3 minutes until the sauce has thickened. For a smoother sauce, simmer over low heat for another 5-10 minutes.

Peanut Sauce

10 minutes

Peanut sauce is what I reach for when I have an episode of "cook's block." Toss it over a grain, such as noodles or rice, and some vegetables for an easy and eternally popular meal. I have successfully made this with sunflower seed butter, if peanut butter is not an option.

$\frac{1}{2}$ **c natural peanut butter**

$\frac{3}{4}$ **c water**

1 T brown sugar

1 t chili sauce

2 t soy sauce

1 T rice vinegar or lime juice

Salt and pepper to taste

Optional: 1 clove garlic, minced

1 t fresh ginger, minced

Blend the ingredients well. Microwave or simmer for 2 to 5 minutes, stirring every 30 seconds. Add ¼ c water to thin further if needed. This can be served as a dipping sauce, or poured over rice, vegetables, noodles, tofu, or meat. Store in the refrigerator for up to two weeks.

Garlic Herb Pizza Sauce

15 minutes active cooking, plus 15 minutes to rest

Pizza sauce freezes very well, and can be frozen in an ice cube tray for cubes that can then be tossed in soup or used individually as needed for pizza or pasta sauce. Pop the cubes out of the tray and store in quart or gallon sized freezer bags. For pasta sauce, add extra vegetables (mushrooms, onions, zucchini, spinach, etc.) or meatballs and more tomato sauce.

Since dried herbs are always available, I specified them, but feel free to use fresh herbs. Add them after the tomato sauce and garlic have simmered together, and cook until just fragrant.

1 T olive oil

3 large cloves garlic, minced

1 small can tomato sauce (8 oz)

1 small can tomato paste (6 oz)

1 T dried oregano

2 t dried thyme

1 T dried basil

1 t dried marjoram

Heat the oil in a small saucepan over medium heat. When it is hot, add the garlic, and stir. Cook until it just starts to turn golden, then stir in the dried herbs. Cook for about 30 seconds, and then add the tomato sauce and tomato paste. Mix well, cover, bring to simmer, and remove from heat. Allow it to rest, covered, for at least 15 minutes. Use immediately, freeze, or refrigerate.

Soups and Salads

Soups and salads are a great way to integrate more vegetables into your eating habits. Most of the dishes here are designed to be whole meal, or they just need a piece of good bread or a muffin on the side. The salads are a blend of classics and unusual combinations. Salads are an easy place to start adapting recipes. Make it your own! The soups take a little longer to make, but mostly they just need to simmer for a few minutes so the flavors can meld. If you use commercial broths, I recommend adding a teaspoon of lemon juice to brighten the flavor.

Summer Salad

Raw Corn, Black Bean, and Fresh Basil Salad

Vegetable Spring Rolls

Sweet Cabbage Apple Salad

Chickpea, Parsley, and Red Pepper Salad

Garlic Soup

Tomato, Broccoli, and Avocado Salad

Sweet Corn Tomato Chowder

Green Bean, Black Olive, and Red Potato Salad

Corn Bean Chowder

Spiced Butternut Squash Soup

Sweet Potato and Black Bean Soup with Lime

Warm Lentil Artichoke Salad

Avoiding waste is a challenging part of planning meals for one. Supermarkets and even farmer's markets can be focused on serving families—making it hard to buy a variety of foods without having some spoil before you can eat them.

> ➤ Shop where you can select the volume of produce. A two-pound bag of green beans is only cheaper if you eat or freeze it all.
> ➤ Buy small perishable items—the smallest cabbage, a Roma tomato, a quart or half gallon of milk.
> ➤ Choose pre-sliced fruit such as melon if you only want a small portion.
> ➤ Visit salad bars for items such as celery or olives when you only need small amounts. Share larger portions (i.e. 2 lb snap peas) with a friend.
> ➤ Freeze extra food ASAP in labeled freezer bags or jars.
> ➤ Incorporate leftovers into dishes like Summer Salad.
> ➤ Cook meals, and freeze those.

Don't forget to eat the food in your freezer every two to three months!

Summer Salad

10 minutes

Possible variations are infinite—add leftover steamed vegetables, herbs, different nuts and seeds, different legumes or leftover grilled fish or meat. Use a different dressing, or neglect a dressing entirely and eat this salad plain.

2 c baby greens or lettuce, washed and coarsely chopped

$\frac{1}{2}$ c chickpeas, drained

$\frac{1}{2}$ c cucumber chunks

1 small tomato, chopped or $\frac{1}{2}$ c red pepper, chopped

$\frac{1}{2}$ c peas, blanched if fresh or thawed if frozen

2 marinated artichoke hearts

1 T vinaigrette (pg. 25)

2 T sunflower or pumpkin seeds

Toss together. Enjoy!

Raw Corn, Black Bean, and Fresh Basil Salad

10 minutes

Raw corn may not sound appealing, but it is crunchy, sweet, and wonderful melded with lime, basil, and sweet bell peppers. Don't use grocery store corn, though; find freshly picked corn from a farmer's market, farm stand, or friend with a farm! Freshly picked corn is sweet while older corn has become starchy.

1 ear corn

$^1/_2$ c cooked or canned black beans, drained

$^1/_2$ c chopped red bell pepper

3 T feta, crumbled

1 T vinaigrette, made with red or white wine vinegar

$^1/_4$ c basil leaves, chopped

1 scallion, white and green parts chopped

2 lime wedges

Optional: 2 T toasted pine nuts

Shuck corn and remove as much silk as possible. Slice the corn off the cob into a bowl. Add the remaining ingredients (except lime) and blend well. Squeeze the lime over the salad immediately before eating.

Vegetable Spring Rolls

10 minutes

What you can include in spring rolls is only limited by your imagination—add leftover steamed vegetables, herbs, or leftover grilled fish or meat. Use a different dressing, or neglect a dressing entirely. Rice paper is often available in major supermarkets, and almost always in Asian groceries.

4 sheets rice paper wrappers

$\frac{1}{4}$ c cucumber, sliced in matchsticks

$\frac{1}{4}$ c carrot, grated

$\frac{1}{4}$ c bean sprouts

$\frac{1}{4}$ c daikon, sliced in matchsticks

1 small bundle rice vermicelli, cooked according to the package

8 stalks basil, cilantro, and/or mint

4 pieces lettuce

Peanut Sauce (pg. 27)

Optional: chives, green beans, mushrooms, onions, spinach

Soak rice paper in cool water (I usually use a pie pan filled with water) until softened. Remove it. Layer the cucumber, carrot, bean sprouts, daikon, and herbs in a line one-third of the way across the sheet. Fold over the narrower edge, fold up the top and bottom, and roll into a bundle. (It's like making a burrito.) Wrap each spring roll in a lettuce leaf with the rice noodles, and dip in the Peanut Sauce.

Variation: Add strips of cooked chicken, tofu, or shrimp.

Sweet Cabbage Apple Salad

10 minutes

Fennel is a surprising vegetable—despite a relatively bland appearance, it packs a serious flavor punch. I recommend using it if you can. Cabbage complements it very nicely in this blend.

2 t mild olive oil

1 t white wine vinegar or lemon juice

Salt and pepper to taste

$\frac{1}{8}$ t sugar, or less

1 c green or red cabbage, sliced thinly and chopped roughly

2 T finely sliced red or white onion

2 T chopped nuts, roasted

3 T raisins

1 small apple, cored and chopped (about $\frac{1}{2}$ c)

$\frac{1}{2}$ small head fennel, thinly sliced (about $\frac{1}{2}$ c)

Mix the olive oil and vinegar together with salt and pepper. Mix the cabbage with the sugar and knead it, pressing and rolling it in a bowl, for two to three minutes. Add all the other ingredients to the cabbage, and top with the dressing.

> **Tip**: If you coat the apple with a little additional lemon juice to prevent browning, this salad will hold well chilled for the next day.

34

Chickpea, Parsley, and Red Pepper Salad

10 minutes

Chickpeas and parsley make a fantastic salad, especially when mixed with sweet crunchy vegetables and briny olives. The original recipe called for carrots, which I still use when red peppers aren't available, but each morsel of red pepper is a crunchy mini-explosion of sweetness. Carrots are good, but not that good.

$\frac{1}{4}$ **clove garlic**

$\frac{1}{4}$ **t dried oregano or 1 T fresh oregano**

2 t olive oil

$\frac{3}{4}$ **t lemon juice**

$\frac{1}{4}$ **t mustard**

1 c coarsely chopped parsley, bottom 2-3" of stem removed

$\frac{2}{3}$ **c cooked or canned chickpeas, drained**

$\frac{1}{2}$ **red bell pepper, diced**

4-5 black olives like Kalamata or Gaeta, coarsely chopped

3 T crumbled feta

Black pepper to taste

Mix the garlic, oregano, olive oil, lemon juice, and mustard to make the dressing. Toss the remaining ingredients together with the dressing. Enjoy!

Garlic Soup

15 minutes

Garlic has a reputation for preventing colds—whether because it has enough antiviral compounds or because people stay a little farther away from you when you've been eating a lot of it. This soup is a great substitute for chicken soup, and it's very easy. Feel free to play with it—use cubes of tofu or fish instead of egg, rice noodles instead of potato, or add a few drops of chili sauce, lime juice, and some greens to it.

3-4 large cloves garlic, peeled and sliced thinly

2 dried mushrooms (any type), broken into pieces

1 c water or broth

1 medium potato, sliced thinly

1 carrot, sliced thinly

1 egg

Salt and pepper to taste

Place the mushroom and garlic with the water in the saucepan over medium high heat. Bring to a boil, and add the carrots. Simmer for 3 minutes, and add the potato. Simmer for another 10 minutes. Meanwhile, break the egg into a bowl and beat well. Mix a tablespoon of hot water from the soup pot to the egg. When the potato is cooked, stir the egg into the soup. Season with salt and pepper to taste. Serve immediately.

Tomato, Broccoli, and Avocado Salad

15 minutes

It works. Try it in late August, when the tomatoes are at their best and it's too hot to do more than steam broccoli.

$1/3$ lb broccoli, washed and cut into florets (½ large crown)

½ ripe avocado, peeled, pitted, and cubed

1 Roma tomato or half of a large tomato

2 t olive oil

1 t lime juice or white wine vinegar (about $1/8$ of a lime)

Salt and pepper to taste

Steam the broccoli in the saucepan, covered, with ½ cup of water for five minutes. While the broccoli is steaming, chop the tomato and avocado. Drain the broccoli and rinse with cold water immediately. Toss with the remaining ingredients.

Variation: Add either $1/4$ c crumbled feta or $1/2$ cooked or canned (drained) black beans.

37

Sweet Corn Tomato Chowder

20 minutes

July or August—when the tomatoes and corn were picked a few short hours before—is when you should make this soup. Freshly picked sweet corn has a supremely sweet and milky flavor on its own. Add a little acidity and fruity notes from the tomatoes, and it yields an excellent soup.

1 shallot, chopped

1 t butter

$\frac{1}{2}$ c fresh or canned tomatoes, diced

$\frac{1}{2}$ bay leaf

$\frac{1}{2}$ c fresh or frozen corn

$\frac{1}{2}$ c milk

$\frac{1}{2}$ t sugar

Salt & pepper to taste

Sauté the shallot in the butter in the saucepan over medium heat, stirring often, until the onion is translucent. Add the tomatoes, bay leaf, salt, and pepper. Simmer for 10 minutes. Add the corn, milk, and sugar. Simmer for another 5 minutes.

How do I know if I'm cooking it right? If you like the way it tastes, you are cooking it right. Just as beauty is in the eye of the beholder, flavor is in the taste buds of the diner.

Green Bean, Black Olive, and Red Potato Salad

20 minutes

This salad is a classic; it can also be a formula: potato topped with protein, green vegetable, and flavorful accompaniments. There are a number of successful variations—add leftover steamed vegetables, herbs, leftover grilled fish or meat, or use a different dressing. It's quite satisfying, and full of healthy fats from the fish and olives.

1 large red potato, washed and cut into eighths

1 c trimmed fresh or frozen green beans

3 oz tuna, canned in olive oil, drained or $\frac{1}{2}$ c white beans, cooked

$\frac{1}{2}$ lemon, juiced

$\frac{1}{3}$ to $\frac{1}{2}$ small red onion, thinly sliced

1 T olive oil

1 T fresh mint (basil or oregano may be substituted), chopped

4 large black olives, such as Kalamata

Boil the potato in a small pot of water for 10 minutes, or until tender. Meanwhile, mix the tuna or white beans, olives, onion, lemon juice, oil, and mint. Remove the potato with the slotted spoon but do not drain the water. Add the green beans to the boiling water in the pot, and cook until tender but slightly crisp (2 minutes for frozen, or 5 for fresh). Meanwhile, place potato on the plate. Drain the green beans and rinse with cold water. Top the potatoes with the green beans and the tuna mixture. Stir together to distribute the dressing, and eat either slightly warm or at room temperature.

Corn Bean Chowder

20 minutes

Like most white chowders, this is reminiscent of frigid New England winters. A few small pieces of pancetta or cubed ham can be added with the onion if you want a meaty flavor.

1 T butter

$\frac{1}{2}$ small onion, minced

$\frac{1}{2}$ stalk celery, minced

1 clove garlic, minced

$\frac{1}{8}$ t thyme

1 T flour

1 c milk (whole milk, or a mixture of milk and cream)

$\frac{1}{3}$ c canned or cooked white beans, drained

$\frac{1}{2}$ c frozen or fresh corn kernels

Salt & pepper to taste

Melt butter in a medium saucepan. Add the onion, celery, and garlic and sauté over medium low heat until translucent. Add the garlic and thyme, and sauté for another two minutes. Increase the heat to medium and add the flour. Stir for two minutes, or until the flour is barely beginning to brown. Whisk in the milk. Stir until the cream base has thickened, then add the beans and corn, and cook over low heat for 10 minutes. Season with salt and pepper to taste.

Spiced Butternut Squash Soup

20 minutes

The lentils are a good source of many nutrients such as iron, folate, and the B vitamins. Cinnamon augments the sweetness of the squash and helps control blood glucose (sugar) levels.

$^2/_3$ c cubed butternut squash

$^1/_4$ c small red lentils

1 clove garlic, trimmed, peeled, and roughly chopped

$^1/_8$ t cinnamon

$^1/_8$ t curry powder

Dash of garam masala

$1^1/_2$ c water or broth

2 T coconut milk

Salt and pepper to taste

Combine all ingredients except the coconut milk in a small saucepan with enough water to cover the squash. Bring to a boil, then simmer for 15 minutes. Puree carefully, add the coconut milk, and thin with additional water or broth if necessary.

Variation: Substitute sweet potato for the butternut squash.

> **Garam Masala** is an Indian spice blend that is readily available in major or gourmet grocers. You can mix your own, but I find it convenient to purchase it rather than the individual spices.

41

Sweet Potato and Black Bean Soup with Lime

25 minutes

Hearty, yet bursting with the fresh flavors of lime and cilantro, this is the perfect late autumn soup. I like it cold in the summer—make it the night before when you're cooking something else and eat it cold for lunch or dinner the next day.

1 T oil

$^1/_2$ small onion, chopped

1 clove garlic, minced

1 t cumin

2 t chili powder

$^1/_8$ t cayenne pepper

$^1/_2$ c sweet potato, peeled and diced ($^1/_4$ medium)

$^1/_3$ c cooked black beans (drained, if canned)

$^2/_3$ c water or broth

$^1/_2$ lime, juiced

1 T chopped cilantro or basil

Sauté the onion in the oil until nearly translucent. Add the garlic and spices and sauté for about a minute. Add the black beans and sweet potatoes, along with enough water or broth to cover. When the sweet potatoes are well cooked, add lime juice to taste and garnish with cilantro.

Warm Lentil Artichoke Salad

40 minutes

Lentils are both a nutrition powerhouse and an affordable pantry basic. French lentils (Du Puy) are particularly good in this salad.

$\frac{1}{4}$ c French green lentils or black beluga lentils

1 bay leaf

1 small shallot, minced

1 small garlic clove, minced

$\frac{1}{8}$ t dried thyme

$\frac{1}{2}$ medium carrot, diced

1 t white wine vinegar or lemon juice

1 t Dijon mustard

1 T olive oil

1 T lentil cooking water

4 marinated artichokes, chopped

Salt and pepper to taste

1 c diced crisp lettuce, like romaine

In a medium saucepan, combine the lentils, 1 c water, bay leaf, shallot, garlic, and thyme. Bring to a boil and simmer for 20 minutes, covered. Add the carrots, cover, and simmer for another 10 minutes or until the lentils are tender. Drain the lentils, reserving a small amount of cooking water. Transfer 1 T cooking water to a medium bowl and whisk in the vinegar, mustard, salt, and pepper. Add the oil in a stream, continuously whisking, until you have a smooth dressing. Toss the lentils in the dressing with the lettuce and artichokes. Serve warm.

Spreads, Dips, and Sandwiches

Spreads and dips are an easy way to incorporate healthy fats and fiber. Unlike the classic potato chip dips, these are primarily based on legumes or vegetables. Each one creates an easy meal with some bread and raw vegetables, and they store reasonably well. I particularly like throwing a spread together while my supper cooks to pack for my lunch the next day.

Roasted Red Pepper Spread

Black Olive Tuna Salad

Lemon Artichoke Salad

Garlicky Carrot Spread

Avocado Egg Salad

English Muffin Pizzas

Zalouk (Eggplant Tomato Spread)

Black Bean Veggie Patties

Earthy Black Olive Lentil Spread

Roasted Red Pepper Spread

5 minutes

Dips and spreads do not need to be made from cream cheese or sour cream. The pureed white beans create a creamy base for a lighter, healthier version still packed with flavor from the red pepper. Raw garlic packs a punch when it is freshly chopped, but it mellows if you prepare the spread in advance.

$\frac{1}{2}$ **c white beans, cooked or canned**

$\frac{1}{4}$ **c diced roasted red pepper**

1 small clove garlic

1-2 stalks fresh basil or oregano

1 T olive oil

Salt and pepper to taste

Optional: 2 T Pecorino Romano, grated

Puree or mash the garlic, herbs, and oil. Add beans and half the red pepper and mash or puree until smooth. Stir in the remaining red pepper, and top with the cheese. Season to taste.

Canned beans are convenient, but tend to be high in sodium. Choose low sodium options, or be sure to both drain and rinse your beans.

Black Olive Tuna Salad

5 minutes

Tuna salad is ubiquitous—but adding a few unusual flavors turns it into a new experience. I prefer tuna canned without oil or water, and highly recommend it over your common chunk light tuna. Finding sustainably fished canned tuna may be challenging, but is worth the effort.

5 oz albacore or Tongol tuna

3 T minced pitted Kalamata olives or flavorful black olive paste

2 T fresh mint

1 T fresh basil, dill, or oregano

1 T balsamic vinegar

2 T olive oil

2 T chives or scallion (green parts as well as white)

Chop tuna and herbs. Mix all ingredients well and enjoy.

Tips for Eating on a Budget

- ➢ Buy whole, unseasoned foods (i.e. plain rice instead of pilaf).
- ➢ Buy dried goods in bulk. Store extra in the freezer to reduce energy use.
- ➢ Freeze extra food from sales or leftovers. Use freezer bags or jars, and label.
- ➢ Use the whole bird (or plant). Greens from vegetables like cauliflower are delicious. Eat the peel, too!
- ➢ Use coupons, but only for the foods you would normally buy.
- ➢ Buy day-old bakery bread and freeze. Toast as needed.
- ➢ Shop at ethnic groceries. Visit wholesale markets.
- ➢ Explore online retailers for specialty items.
- ➢ Garden. Even a pot of spinach or herbs on the windowsill helps.

Finally, don't skimp on basic nutrition. Feeding yourself well will improve your quality of life and future health. Eating your greens today may help keep diabetes or osteoporosis away. Seek assistance if you need it. Many adults need food assistance during their lives, and **food is a human right**.

Lemon Artichoke Spread

5 minutes

The combination of lemon and artichoke is sublime. I'll happily eat if off a spoon, but it's also quite good with bread, crackers, carrot sticks, cucumber slices, asparagus spears, and so on!

$^1\!/_2$ c cooked or canned white beans

6 oz (small jar) marinated artichoke hearts, drained

1 T fresh oregano or 1 t dried oregano

2 T lemon juice or white wine vinegar

1 T olive oil

Salt & pepper to taste

Optional: pinch of cayenne pepper

Puree beans, oregano, artichoke hearts, lemon juice, and cayenne pepper, if using. Thin to the desired consistency with the olive oil, drizzling it in slowly. Season to taste with salt and pepper.

Garlicky Carrot Spread

10 minutes

Inspired by my first taste of *skordalia* at the bar of a trendy restaurant, this has a strong garlic bite when freshly made. Try it on sandwiches, crackers, or broiled lamb chops; with raw vegetables, or on triangles of pita bread. After 24 hours, it mellows and can be thinned with broth to make a soup instead.

3 medium carrots, well-scrubbed but not peeled

2 small cloves garlic

$\frac{1}{4}$ c hard cheese like Parmesan, grated

1 T red or white wine vinegar

2 t dried oregano or 2 T fresh oregano

1 t dried thyme

2 T olive oil

Chop carrots into chunks and steam in a few tablespoons of water until well done (in the microwave or on the stove). Reserve the cooking water. Place garlic and $\frac{1}{3}$ c carrot cooking water into a blender or food processor and blend well. Add the herbs, oil, carrots, and vinegar and blend until smooth. Add more cooking water if necessary. Blend in the cheese, and serve immediately.

Avocado Egg Salad

10 minutes

You'll want to use a very ripe avocado for the best results here. Ripe avocados have a hint of softness, but the skin should not feel loose. If the avocado is not very ripe, you may need to add a tablespoon of olive oil. Either way, this twist on egg salad is chock full of good fats and protein.

1 hard-boiled egg, chopped

$\frac{1}{2}$ avocado, peeled, pitted, and chopped

$\frac{1}{8}$ t cayenne pepper (or less, to taste)

$\frac{1}{4}$ small onion, finely chopped

1 T parsley, finely chopped

1 t white wine vinegar

Salt and pepper to taste

Mix all the ingredients by hand, mashing slightly, until well blended. Serve cool, in sandwiches or as you would egg salad.

English Muffin Pizzas

20 minutes

If you haven't had one since you attended or hosted a grade school birthday party, try it again. They are a perfect size, and make a full healthy meal with steamed vegetables or a salad. The healthier version uses whole grain English muffins with part-skim mozzarella.

1 English muffin

2-4 T pizza or tomato sauce

$\frac{1}{4}$ c grated mozzarella

2 t Parmesan or pecorino romano

Pinch oregano

2 T pizza toppings: green pepper, olives, tomato, pepperoni, etc.

Preheat oven (or toaster oven) to 400°F. Spread the English muffin with the pizza sauce and top with cheese, oregano, and toppings. Bake for 10 minutes at 400°F, or in a toaster oven until the cheese is melted.

Variation: Use corn tortillas or an arepa instead of the English muffin.

> **Pizza Sauce** goes from bland to brilliant with just a few additions. Try Garlic Herb Pizza Sauce, pg. 28.

Zalouk (Eggplant Tomato Spread)

35 minutes

The classic combination of eggplant and tomatoes not only makes great pasta dishes, but also a refrigerator staple with a North African twist. Use it to create a vegetable stuffed pita, or serve as a dip with crackers.

1 c eggplant, peeled and cut into $\frac{1}{2}$" cubes ($\frac{1}{2}$ small eggplant)

1 T olive oil

1 medium ripe tomato, chopped

1 clove garlic, minced

1 T parsley, chopped

Pinch cayenne or ground chili pepper

1 T lemon juice

Salt & pepper to taste

Steam the eggplant for 10 minutes to soften. Meanwhile, chop the tomatoes, garlic, and parsley. Drain the eggplant and set aside. Heat the oil in the saucepan and add the garlic, parsley, chili pepper, and tomato. Simmer for 10 minutes. Add the eggplant, and simmer for another 5 minutes. Mash lightly with a spoon, stir in the lemon juice, and season to taste.

Black Bean Veggie Patties

35 minutes

Making your own veggie burgers isn't all that much trouble and they taste much better than what you find commercially. If you're going to get the food processor dirty *and* use the oven, I say make extra and freeze them. This recipe makes six, depending on size.

1 shallot, peeled and cut into 1" chunks

1 carrot, cut into 1" chunks

1 c cooked or canned black beans, drained

$\frac{1}{2}$ c corn, fresh or frozen

$\frac{1}{2}$ c spinach, blanched or frozen, drained well

4 T cornmeal

1 T chili powder

1 T dried oregano

2 t cumin

1 egg

Salt & pepper to taste

Process the shallot and carrot in a food processor until finely ground. Add the remaining ingredients to the food processor and process until well mixed. Spoon onto an oiled griddle or frying pan over medium high heat. Cook for 4-6 minutes on each side. Alternatively, broil for 4 minutes on each side.

No food processor? Chop all ingredients finely and mash with the egg.

Earthy Black Olive Lentil Spread

50 minutes

Another spread featuring healthy fats from olives, this delicious combination is also a great source of fiber and iron. It takes longer than most other recipes if you are cooking the lentils from scratch, but it freezes well and can be stored in the refrigerator for one week. This makes approximately 3 cups.

$^2/_3$ **c dry brown lentils**

1 bay leaf

1 t thyme

1 clove garlic, peeled

$^1/_4$ **t cayenne pepper**

2 T lemon juice

$^1/_2$ **c pitted black olives, such as Alphonse or Kalamata**

2–4 T olive oil

Salt and pepper to taste

Cook lentils with bay leaf, garlic, and thyme in plenty of water for 40 minutes or until tender. Drain and remove the bay leaf. Puree the lentils with the olives, lemon juice, and cayenne pepper until smooth. Thin with olive oil until it reaches a consistency between cream cheese and sour cream. Eat on hearty bread as a sandwich, or thin further and use as a dip for raw vegetables.

Vegetables, Beans, and Grains

One of the tricks of cooking for one is to focus on one-pot meals. Otherwise, the dishes can quickly become overwhelming. The following dishes are either complete meals, or simply need a piece of toast, bowl of rice, or a few carrot sticks to turn it into a sound supper.

Technique: Cooking Grains

Technique: Cooking Vegetables

Cheesy Navy Beans

The Locally Produced Microwave Burrito

Garlicky Broccoli Raab over Polenta

Sweet Potato with Spicy Black Beans

Greens in Cheese Sauce

Algerian Carrots and Chickpeas

Creamy Cauliflower with White Beans

Quick Quinoa Kale Salad

Spicy Cabbage and Tofu with Noodles

Creamy Cauliflower Carrot Custard

Technique: Cooking Grains

"The staff of life" is not just bread, but also wheat, pasta, kasha, rice, quinoa, millet, cous-cous, and myriad other forms of grains. Grains store very well, making them an essential part of a single person's kitchen. Keep whole grains that you won't use within a few months in the fridge or freezer to prevent moth infestations and/or rancidity. Quick cooking grains are relatively cheap, usually make for good leftovers, and freeze well.

In general, follow the instructions on the package. Whole grains may be rinsed, but do not rinse any enriched grains such as white rice or cornmeal. Stir the grain into cold or boiling water (or stock). Bring the grain and water to a boil, reduce the heat to low, cover, and simmer until the grain is cooked. If necessary, add a little more water at the end. Avoid stirring, if possible. When the grain is cooked, stir to fluff and add any butter or oil. Cover again and let rest for 5 minutes before serving. Polenta, unlike other grains, should be cooked uncovered and stirred often to develop its creaminess.

Grain	Grain to Water Ratio	Time (min)	Start with…
Barley	1:3.5	60	Cold water
Brown Rice	1:2	45	Cold water
Bulgur	1:2	20	Cold water
Cous-Cous	1:1.25	5-10	Boiling water
Kasha	1:2	15	Boiling water
Millet	1:3	35	Cold water
Polenta	1:4	25	Boiling water
Quinoa	1:2	20	Cold water
White Rice	1:2	18	Cold water
Wild Rice	1:3	45-60	Cold water

Technique: Cooking Vegetables

Steamed: Cover the bottom of a saucepan with ½" water. Insert your steamer basket, if you use one. (Steamer baskets produce more evenly cooked vegetables, but the difference between using one and not using one is very small.) Add diced or trimmed vegetables. Cover tightly, and place over high heat until the water begins to boil, about 1 minute. Turn heat to medium low. Do not remove the lid until just before the end of the cooking time. Test by tasting or stabbing with a fork. Drain, reserving the steaming water to use as broth if desired.

Blanched: Bring a large pot of water to a full roiling boil. Immerse the vegetables, and then remove promptly with tongs or a strainer, dropping into a bowl of ice water. Generally, aim to leave leafy or tender vegetables in the boiling water for 30 seconds to 1 min., and firmer vegetables like broccoli and green beans in the boiling water for 1–2 min. If you are freezing them, drain well before packing in freezer bags.

> Blanched vegetables in vinaigrette often hold better than dressed salads if you're making it ahead of time. See the Dressings and Sauces chapter for a vinaigrette recipe. Feel free to play with the recipe by using new oils or seasonings.

Boiled: Immerse vegetables in a pot of boiling water. For root vegetables, begin with cold water and bring to a boil. Drain when tender or soft, as needed.

Dried Beans & Peas: Soak in water for 8–12 hours. Simmer for 60–90 minutes, or until soft. Alternatively, bring to a boil. Remove from the heat and soak for two hours. Simmer for 60–90 minutes, or until soft.

Roasted: Toss in oil and bake in a single layer at 400°F, turning every 10–15 minutes, until soft.

Vegetable Cooking Times

Times are approximate, as the size of the pieces, the age of the vegetables, and whether you want them crisp, tender, or soft affects the cooking times. In general, smaller pieces and younger items cook faster. Items without steaming times are best boiled or roasted.

Vegetable	Steam (min)	Boil (min)
Asparagus	4	4
Beans, green	7	5
Beets	--	25–45
Broccoli	7	5
Brussels Sprouts	10	6
Cabbage	10	8
Carrots	15	10
Cauliflower	7	5
Collards	12	8
Corn on the Cob	15	4
Greens, tender	5	4
Kale	10	7
Parsnip	15	10
Peas	5	4
Potatoes	--	15
Sweet Potatoes	--	15
Turnips	--	20
Winter Squash	25	20
Yellow Squash	7	5
Zucchini	7	5

Cheesy Navy Beans

8 minutes

One of my fastest to prepare suppers, you can make this under the broiler or in the microwave. Add some good bread and a piece of fruit for dessert, and you have an excellent quick meal. I like using an oven-safe dish or a French onion soup bowl.

1 c cooked or canned cannellini
  or navy beans, drained
$\frac{1}{4}$ t dried mustard
$\frac{1}{4}$ t dried thyme
$\frac{1}{4}$ c milk
$\frac{1}{4}$ c grated extra sharp
  Cheddar or strong
  Swiss cheese
Salt and pepper to taste

Mix the beans with the mustard, thyme, salt and pepper to taste in a small casserole dish. Moisten with the milk, and mash slightly. Top with the cheese and microwave for 2 minutes, or until the cheese has melted. Broil for 2–3 minutes for a browned top, if desired.

What makes this a healthy alternative to Mac and Cheese?

This version substitutes beans for the butter and white pasta. Beans and peas are great sources of fiber, so you eat fiber instead of fat and refined starches from the white pasta and butter. The fiber helps:

➢ keep you full
➢ regulate your blood glucose (sugar) levels
➢ smooth out your digestive process
➢ lower cholesterol
➢ control weight

Research supports eating naturally occurring fiber, like the type in beans, whole grains, fruit, and vegetables. Added fiber may or may not have the same positive impact on your health.

The Locally Produced Microwave Burrito

10 minutes

I had friends in college who subsisted on frozen burritos and cereal. Making your own only takes a few extra minutes, and tastes considerably better. Oh, and they are more economical.

$\frac{1}{3}$ **c black beans**

3 T salsa or chopped tomato

1 large tortilla or 2 small tortillas

$\frac{1}{4}$ **cup diced red and/or green pepper**

1 handful washed fresh spinach (about 1 cup)

1 oz Monterey Jack cheese

Optional: $\frac{1}{4}$ **c cooked corn or rice**

               2 T chopped or sliced olives

               2–3 slices chili pepper

               2–3 scallions, green and white, chopped

               2 T guacamole

               2 T sour cream or plain yogurt

Mash the black beans in a bowl with the back of a spoon. Add the salsa and spinach. Microwave, covered, for about 2 minutes or until the spinach is wilted. Spoon into a tortilla with the cheese and add any vegetables and rice. Heat again briefly (about 30 seconds) to melt the cheese. Serve with any cold accompaniments desired.

Garlicky Broccoli Raab over Polenta

15 minutes

Broccoli raab tends to be pricey in the supermarket, but it's very easy to grow. Set a pot on your porch, or in a kitchen window.

¼ c finely ground cornmeal

1 c water

¼ t salt

¼ lb broccoli raab, washed and cut into 2" lengths

1 T olive oil

1 clove garlic

Pinch of red pepper flakes

½ t oregano

Optional: Parmesan, to taste

Stir together the cornmeal, salt, and water in a microwaveable bowl. Let sit for 3–5 minutes. Heat the oil in a small saucepan. Add the garlic and herbs and stir for 30 seconds. Add the broccoli raab and sauté for 2 minutes. Meanwhile, microwave the cornmeal mixture for 5 minutes, stirring well every 30 seconds, and adding more water if necessary. Add a few tablespoons of water to broccoli raab, cover, and steam for 4–5 minutes or until tender. Pour the broccoli raab over the polenta and top with grated cheese if desired. For a more refined dish, mix the vegetables with the polenta in a pie pan and broil until toasted on the top.

Variation: Substitute other greens or mushrooms for the broccoli raab.

Sweet Potato with Spicy Black Beans

15 minutes

When you mix the beans with spices, you are essentially making refried beans. Mash them slightly if you like, or use plain beans if you're too hungry to wait.

1 medium sweet potato

$^1/_2$ c black beans or pinto beans

3 T chopped onion

1 T olive oil

$^1/_2$ t chili powder

Optional: 2 slices Monterey Jack cheese

2 T salsa

Wash sweet potato well and stab with a fork several times. Microwave until done (4–8 minutes), flipping every couple of minutes. Meanwhile, heat the oil in a small pan over high heat and add the onion. Stir for 2–3 minutes, then add the chili powder. After the chili powder has become fragrant, add the beans and salsa. Heat through. Remove the potato from the microwave and slice open. Pour the beans over, and top with the cheese. Microwave for about 30 seconds to melt the cheese, if desired.

Variation: Add $^1/_2$ c cooked broccoli, chopped peppers, spinach, corn, or a blend of the above.

Greens in Cheese Sauce

20 minutes

Greens are as nutritious as Popeye would have you believe. When you want something a little decadent, toss them with a flavorful cheese sauce. I particularly like using chard and kale for this recipe, but spinach and cabbage work well too.

$\frac{1}{2}$ **bunch (8 oz) greens, washed, stemmed, and chopped**

1 T butter

1 T flour

$\frac{1}{2}$ **small onion, chopped**

1 clove garlic, minced

$\frac{2}{3}$ **c milk**

2 oz sharp cheddar, grated

1 slice toast (or rice, pasta, etc.)

Place the greens in a large covered saucepan over medium high heat. If they are still wet from being washed, do not add water. Otherwise, add a few tablespoons of water and steam, until barely wilted. Remove and drain well.

Melt the butter in the saucepan. Add the onion and garlic and cook until the onion is translucent. Add the flour and stir until barely toasted, then whisk in the milk. When the sauce thickens, lower the heat to low and stir in the greens and cheese. When the cheese has melted, serve immediately as a side dish or over toast.

Variation: Substitute sautéed mushrooms for the cooked greens.

Algerian Carrots and Chickpeas

20 minutes

Fragrant with the scents of North African souks, this simple dish makes carrots an entirely new experience. Eat over cous-cous for an authentic meal, or with pita bread and Zalouk (pg. 52).

1 T olive oil

1 clove garlic, minced

$1^1\!/_2$ t cumin

$^1\!/_4$ t paprika

$^1\!/_8$ t salt

$^1\!/_3$ c water

2 carrots, halved lengthwise and sliced horizontally

$^2\!/_3$ c cooked or canned chickpeas

Heat the oil in a saucepan. Stir in the garlic and spices. After the garlic is fragrant (about 30 seconds), add the carrots, water, and chickpeas. Bring to a boil and reduce the heat. Simmer for 15 minutes or until the carrots are tender and the water has evaporated.

Variation: Add 2 T raisins with the chickpeas.

Tips for Quick Cooking

Meal planning and cooking ahead are particularly helpful if you tend to be crunched for time.

> Prepare as much in advance as possible: sliced onions, spreads, chopped vegetables, cooked grains, salad dressing, etc.
> Use a food processor if you are a slow slicer and dicer.
> Skip peeling. Cooked vegetable skins are often nutritious and palatable.
> Keep your kitchen organized and stocked. Store items in the same place.
> Clean up after yourself as you cook.
> Buy frozen or precut vegetables if your budget allows.
> Keep some cooked rice or other grain in your freezer.
> Store a few back-up meals in the freezer.
> Cook two things at once.

Some meals that reheat well include Algerian Carrots and Chickpeas, Sweet Potato and Black Bean Soup with Lime, Cheesy Navy Beans, Spiced Butternut Soup, and Individual Spinach Frittatas.

Creamy Cauliflower with White Beans

20 minutes

The combination of creamy white beans and tender-crisp cauliflower with light seasoning is delightful. Go easy on the hot pepper flakes—this shouldn't be a spicy dish, there should be just a hint of spice to perk it up. Enjoy it alone, with meat or fish, or over your favorite grain.

1 T olive oil

$\frac{1}{2}$ small onion, finely chopped

$\frac{1}{4}$ small cauliflower, trimmed and cut into small florets

$\frac{1}{2}$ c canned or cooked white beans

$\frac{1}{4}$ t dried oregano

$\frac{1}{8}$ t cumin

Pinch of hot pepper flakes

Salt and pepper to taste

Optional: 1 clove garlic, minced

Sauté the onion in the oil until nearly translucent. Add the garlic, oregano, cumin, and hot pepper. Stir for 30 seconds, then add the cauliflower florets and $\frac{1}{4}$ c of water. Cover tightly, and let steam for 5 minutes. Add the beans, cover, and simmer for 5 minutes. Stir occasionally, adding additional water if you prefer a soupier consistency.

Quick Quinoa Kale Salad

20 minutes

Kale is a nutrition powerhouse, but sometimes a little bitter. Balanced with the earthy quinoa, sharp onion, salty chickpeas, and sweet raisins, it's perfect.

1$\frac{1}{2}$ c blanched or steamed kale, chopped

$\frac{1}{3}$ c black quinoa

$\frac{2}{3}$ c water

$\frac{1}{4}$ t dried sage

$\frac{1}{2}$ t dried thyme

3 T diced red onion

4 t white wine vinegar

2 T olive oil

$\frac{1}{2}$ c canned* chickpeas, drained

$\frac{1}{4}$ c raisins

Salt and black pepper to taste

Defrost or prepare the kale. Cook the quinoa in the water. Meanwhile, mix together the herbs, onion, vinegar, and oil to make the dressing. When the quinoa is done (taste it!), toss with the kale, chickpeas, dressing, and raisins. Allow to cool for at least 5 minutes, preferably until room temperature.

Variation: Substitute wild rice for the quinoa.

*If you are using homemade chickpeas, add a little extra salt.

Spicy Cabbage and Tofu with Noodles

20 minutes

Even in deep winter when other greens are limp and sad, cabbage tends to look robust and fresh. It's also a nice frugal purchase for those times when the budget is tight, or there's a lot of unexpected company.

$\frac{1}{8}$ **small head cabbage, chopped**

$\frac{1}{2}$ **onion, chopped**

$\frac{1}{2}$ **carrot, sliced**

4 oz tofu, cut into bite-sized pieces

2 oz Asian rice noodles

2 T vegetable oil

1 clove garlic, minced

1 T soy sauce

Optional: 2 t chili garlic sauce

Dash toasted sesame oil

Soak the noodles as the package directs for a stir-fry and set aside. Mix the chili sauce, sesame oil (if using), and soy sauce into $\frac{1}{4}$ c water and set aside. Heat the oil until hot in large skillet over medium high heat. Add the tofu and brown lightly on each side. Remove from pan and set aside. Stir the onion into the pan, and then add the carrot and garlic. Stir over high heat for about 2 minutes. Add $\frac{1}{4}$ c water and the cabbage, cover, lower heat, and allow the cabbage to steam for about 3 minutes. Stir in the noodles, tofu, and soy sauce mixture. Mix well, and cook until all ingredients are tender and heated through.

Creamy Cauliflower Carrot Custard

35 minutes

One of my favorite dishes has long been a carrot cauliflower quiche. I made it into a simple vegetable custard for an everyday meal. The sweetness and creaminess of the evaporated milk adds a richness that compensates for the lack of a crust, and adds a hint of sweetness.

$\frac{1}{4}$ **c diced carrot (about half a carrot)**

1 c finely chopped cauliflower (about $\frac{1}{6}$ head of cauliflower)

$\frac{1}{4}$ **t dried marjoram**

Pinch black mustard seeds

1 T Pecorino Romano

$\frac{1}{4}$ **c evaporated milk**

1 large egg

1 T extra sharp cheddar or strong Swiss cheese

Preheat oven to 325°F. Steam the cauliflower and carrot until very tender, almost soft. Drain. Toss the cauliflower and carrots with the marjoram, mustard seeds, and Pecorino Romano. Place the vegetables in a two-cup baking dish or custard cup. Meanwhile, beat the egg and evaporated milk together. Pour the egg mixture over the vegetables. Top with the cheddar. For silken edges, place your baking dish in a larger dish with about 1" hot water. If you don't mind browned edges, skip the water bath. Bake for 20–25 minutes, or until the center is firm.

Fish and Meat

Fish and meat tend to fill the protein section of the American plate. Search for sustainably produced options, as the environmental and health impacts of non-sustainable production can be quite devastating. In addition, animals fed on grass, or wild caught fish, generally have healthier fat profiles and taste better.

These recipes use small amounts of meat and fish, and most can be easily adapted to be vegetarian.

Technique: Cooking Meat and Fish

[Protein] Creole on Rice

Quinoa and Tuna with Peanut Sauce

Salmon Artichoke Patties

Plum Duck Breast

Wheels with Spicy Sausage and Broccoli

Pasta with Spinach, Peas, and Salmon

Jeweled Rice and Tuna Pilaf

Technique: Cooking Meat and Fish

Cooking meats and fish can be challenging for the single cook. Take, for example, the most economical form of poultry: a whole bird. It's a bit much for one person, even if you start with a roasted chicken and end with soup. The simplest option for the cook on a budget who is not interested in breaking down a whole chicken into pieces is to simply view meat as a luxury to be eaten occasionally. A friendly butcher or meat department manager can also help by packaging smaller amounts appropriate for one. Some cuts particularly friendly to single cooks include:

- lamb and pork chops
- fish fillets and steaks
- small beef steaks
- chicken and duck breasts
- beef or lamb cubed for stew.

Always check the dates on the packages before buying, and chose meat that has not been previously frozen if you plan to freeze it. If it has been previously frozen, cook it before refreezing to maintain meat quality and safety.

Safe Kitchen Practices

Food poisoning, unfortunately, is a common experience. The USDA recently tested supermarket chickens and found that 100% carried bacteria that cause food-borne illnesses. Following safe practices at home is one easy step toward protecting yourself.

- Refrigerate or freeze immediately upon arriving home.
- Keep your refrigerator below 40°F.
- Separate raw meats, poultry, and fish from other foods in the refrigerator and while cooking.
- Use a separate cutting board for raw meats, poultry, and fish.
- Cook thoroughly. Consult the USDA for the most current recommendations on internal temperatures.
- Check temperatures with a thermometer.
- Place leftovers in the refrigerator or freezer promptly.
- Use 2 c water with 1 t bleach or a steam cleaner to sterilize cutting boards and counters.

Cooking Methods

Braise: Season as desired. Brown the food by cooking it over high heat in fat before braising it. Place in a shallow pan with a small amount of liquid, and cook, covered. Keep the liquid at a simmer.

Broil: Season as desired. Place under a preheated broiler and broil for 3–5 minutes per inch of chop, steak, or fillet. Flip, and broil approximately 3–5 minutes or until the internal temperature reaches the minimum necessary.

Poach: Season the fish or poultry as desired. Heat the poaching liquid (broth, wine, cider, etc.) and add the fish or poultry when it reaches a simmer. Simmer until cooked through, or approximately 5 minutes per pound of fish or 8 minutes for a chicken breast.

Sauté: Season as desired. Heat a skillet over medium heat and coat the bottom with oil or butter. Add the meat, poultry, or fish and gently stir or flip occasionally. Cook for 5–15 minutes, depending on the size, or until fish barely flakes and meats are cooked through.

Stew: Toss the stew meat with a little flour seasoned with salt and pepper. Heat oil in a medium pot over medium high heat. Add the meat and brown. When it has browned, add cubed vegetables such as onion, shallots, celery, carrots, or potatoes. Cover the mixture with a flavorful broth and herbs or spices. Cook over low heat until the meat and vegetables are tender.

When is it done?

Pull out that meat thermometer! Whole cuts of meat, like pork chops or roasts, should be cooked to 145°F and allowed to rest for at least 3 minutes before eating. If you like it well done, cook to 160°F. Ground meat should be cooked to 160°F. Any form of poultry (whole or ground) should reach 165°F, and fish is fully cooked but not dry around 140°F (tuna can benefit from being removed from the heat around 125°F).

[Protein] Creole on Rice

10 minutes

Shrimp work particularly well in this recipe, but you can also try scallops, chicken, pork, a poached egg*, or gigantes (giant white beans). Serve over toast or pasta if you prefer.

2 t olive oil

4 T onion, diced

2 T chopped green bell pepper, diced

2 T celery, diced

Dash cayenne pepper

$\frac{1}{4}$ lb peeled shrimp or other protein, cut in bite-sized pieces

$\frac{1}{4}$ c garlic herb pizza sauce (pg. 28)

1 c cooked rice

Salt & black pepper to taste

Heat oil in a sauté pan. Cook the onion, peppers, and celery until the onion is translucent. Stir to prevent sticking. Add the cayenne pepper and shrimp (or other protein). Toss until the shrimp are barely pink, or your protein is just cooked. Remove the shrimp/protein from the pan. Add the pizza sauce to the pan and stir until simmering. Season to taste. Return the shrimp or other protein to the pan. Meanwhile, heat the rice. Serve shrimp and sauce over the rice.

*Poach the egg separately. Serve it on the rice, topped with the vegetables in the tomato sauce.

73

Quinoa and Tuna with Peanut Sauce

20 minutes

Quinoa was recognized as a "superfood" several years ago because it contains all the amino acids (protein molecules) essential for human health; it is now readily available but it has also become more expensive. If you like this recipe, try it using millet or rice. Even with slightly less nutritious grains, this is close to a perfect one-pot meal with protein, grain, green vegetable, orange vegetable, and healthy fats.

$\frac{1}{4}$ **c quinoa**

$\frac{1}{2}$ **onion, chopped**

2 T oil

1 carrot, sliced

1 c broccoli florets

1 clove garlic, minced

1–2 t chili sauce, or to taste

$\frac{1}{2}$ **lime, juiced**

1 t soy sauce

1 T peanut butter

3 oz cooked or canned tuna, or 3 oz cubed firm tofu

Sauté the onion in the oil until nearly translucent. Add the carrot and garlic and stir for about one minute, then add the quinoa and $1\frac{1}{2}$ c of water. Cover and simmer for 10 minutes. Stir in the broccoli and cover again. Add a little additional water if the quinoa appears to be sticking. Mix the peanut butter, chili sauce, soy sauce, lime juice, and 3 T of hot water. When the broccoli is tender, add the peanut sauce and tuna. Enjoy!

Variation: Substitute cooked pork, chicken, or beef for the tuna.

Salmon Artichoke Patties

20 minutes

This is a pantry staples recipe for me! Artichokes are a great source of antioxidants. They complement the rich salmon very nicely, and help increase your vegetable intake when mixed into the burgers. I like to serve them with lemon wedges and plenty of mustard, and they are good either hot or cold.

Buy wild salmon if possible, as it tends to be higher in the omega-3 fats, and farmed salmon often does not have the beneficial nutrients of wild salmon. Canned salmon with bones adds calcium to your diet, but you need to mash the bones. It's fairly easy to mash them between the back of a spoon, or the flat of a knife, and a cutting board.

6 oz canned salmon, drained and chopped

6 oz marinated artichokes, drained and minced

2 t cornmeal

1 large egg

$\frac{1}{4}$ t oregano flakes or dill weed

Optional: Pinch chili flakes

Mix all ingredients until well blended. Shape into small patties $1\frac{1}{2}$" in diameter and $\frac{1}{2}$" thick. Cook over medium low heat on an oiled or non-stick griddle for about 6 minutes per side. Flip when the color on the edges begins to lighten, or when they are browned. Cook for another 5–6 minutes, and remove from the pan. Serve warm or cold.

Plum Duck Breast

20 minutes

Duck breast is conveniently packaged for one. If you find one to be too large, reserve a few of the cooked slices to add to a salad or stir-fry the next day. Enjoy this plain, with a salad or steamed vegetables, or serve it over rice or cous-cous.

1 boneless duck breast

Salt & pepper to taste

$\frac{1}{4}$ c broth or dry red wine

1 T plum or apricot preserves

2 T chopped or slivered almonds, toasted

Heat a sauté pan over medium heat. Lightly salt and pepper the duck breast. Place it skin side down on the pan. In about 8 minutes, when the breast is done releasing its fat, drain the excess fat and flip the breast. Cook for another 8 minutes and remove from the pan to a cutting board. Add the broth or wine to the pan along with the preserves and stir, scraping up the brown bits from the bottom. Simmer for about 2 minutes, while you slice the duck breast. Remove the skin, if desired. Spoon the sauce over the duck, and top with toasted almonds.

Always insert a meat thermometer into the thickest part of the breast, chop, fillet, etc.

Wheels with Spicy Sausage and Broccoli

25 minutes

My butcher makes his own sausage on Thursdays. And, to my pleasure, he will sell me a single sausage without blinking. They often end up in a pasta and greens dish, like this. This can be topped with cheese, if you like.

$1\frac{1}{2}$ oz pasta, wheels or other fun shape

1 hot Italian sausage (if mild, add $\frac{1}{4}$ t red pepper flakes)

1 clove garlic, minced

1 c trimmed broccoli

1 small onion, diced

$\frac{1}{2}$ t dried basil

$\frac{1}{4}$ c pasta cooking water or broth

Optional: 1 Roma tomato, diced

Bring water to a boil for the pasta. Add pasta to the water. Three minutes before the pasta is scheduled to be done, add the broccoli to the pot. Drain when both are done, reserving a small amount of water.

Meanwhile, cook the sausage over medium heat with the onion. When cooked through, remove the sausage to a cutting board and slice. Drain extra fat from the pan. Add the garlic and basil to the onion, and return the sausage pieces to the pot. After 1–2 minutes, add the pasta and tomato (if using). Drizzle in a small amount of the pasta cooking water, to create a sauce. Serve immediately.

Variation: Substitute 1 cup cooked lentils or white beans for the pasta.

Pasta with Spinach, Peas, and Salmon

25 minutes

Wild Alaskan salmon is both healthier and more sustainable than farmed fish. I find that canned is most readily available, but feel free to broil fresh salmon or use smoked salmon for another flavor.

2 oz spiral pasta

1 T olive oil

$\frac{1}{2}$ small onion, diced

1 clove garlic, minced

1 t oregano

1 t basil

Pinch cayenne pepper

$\frac{1}{2}$ c peas, fresh or frozen

$1\frac{1}{2}$ c frozen spinach (defrosted) or 3 c fresh spinach

3 oz canned or cooked salmon, flaked and drained

Parmesan cheese to taste

Bring a large pot of water to a boil. Meanwhile, chop the onion and mince the garlic. Cook pasta until tender. Drain, reserving about 1 cup pasta cooking water. In the same pot, add the oil and onion. Cook, stirring over medium high heat, until the onion is almost translucent. Stir in the garlic, herbs, and cayenne. Cook for about 30 seconds. Mix in the peas, spinach, 2–3 T pasta cooking water, and pasta. Lower to a medium heat, and cover for 3 minutes, or until the spinach is cooked. Toss with the salmon and cheese. If needed, add additional reserved water. Serve warm or hot.

Jeweled Rice and Tuna Pilaf

15 to 50 minutes

Using precooked rice means you lose a little flavor from toasting the rice, but you save a substantial amount of time. This works in the rice cooker too.

1 shallot, diced

1 T olive oil

1 clove garlic, minced

1 t dried oregano

1 small carrot, diced

$\frac{1}{2}$ c fresh or frozen peas

3 oz tuna, drained or $\frac{1}{2}$ c chickpeas, drained

$\frac{1}{4}$ c uncooked rice or $\frac{3}{4}$ c cooked rice

Salt and pepper to taste

Olive oil, to taste

Optional: 5 cherry tomatoes, quartered

Heat 1 T oil over medium heat and add the shallot. Cook, stirring occasionally, until the onion is translucent. Add the garlic and oregano, and then stir in the carrots and rice.

Cooked rice: Add remaining ingredients and heat through. Season with olive oil, salt, and pepper and serve warm.

Uncooked rice: Stir for 3 to 5 minutes, until the rice begins to toast (it will be slightly opaque, rather than brown). Add $\frac{1}{2}$ cup water and cover. Bring to a boil, then turn the heat to low, cover, and simmer for 20 minutes (white rice) or 45 minutes (brown rice). Add remaining ingredients. Stir well, and heat through. Drizzle with the additional olive oil and season with salt and pepper.

Desserts

Much like coffee or tea at the end of the meal, dessert can be an excuse to linger with friends over the table, or simply an enjoyable way to end a meal. Homemade desserts are a great way to add a bit more fruit, dairy, or protein to a meal. Focus on simple everyday desserts with intense flavors, made from fruit, dairy, or whole grains instead of white flour, fat, and sugar. Make some tea or coffee, light a candle, and relax!

Dark Hot Cocoa

Plum Compote

Zesty Berries with Whipped Ricotta

Spiced Baked Apple

Rice Pudding

Chocolate Covered Cherries

Pears and Cheese

Dark Hot Cocoa

5 minutes

Hot cocoa is often thought to be a treat reserved for kids or the adults who built snowmen with them, but it's a simple way to end a meal with a touch of sweetness (and an extra serving of milk). This version ups the cocoa and decreases the sugar to emphasize the chocolate. You can also make it an "adult" beverage by adding a dash of rum or peppermint schnapps (without the cinnamon).

2 heaping T cocoa

2 t sugar

Dash of cinnamon

1 c milk

Optional: 2 T whipped cream

Stir the cocoa, cinnamon, and sugar together in a large mug. Add 4 T milk and stir until the cocoa is moist. Microwave for 15–30 seconds. Stir until smooth. Add remaining milk and heat until pleasingly hot. Top with whipped cream, if desired.

Plum Compote

15 minutes

Plums are sometimes underappreciated in the United States. On my last trip to Germany, I ate a series of delicious plum cakes and tarts. Since then, I've worked on finding simple ways to capture those flavors without making an entire cake. This easy compote is one of my favorites—serve it cold over ice cream, warm over spice cake, or plain, garnished with a wafer cookie.

4 very ripe prune (Italian) plums

2–3 pieces candied ginger

$\frac{1}{8}$ t cinnamon

1 T dark rum

Optional: 1 T sugar

Wash the plums. Pit and coarsely chop them. Mince the candied ginger. Place all the ingredients in a saucepan and bring to a boil. Simmer, stirring occasionally, for 5–10 minutes. This can be refrigerated for 3–5 days.

Zesty Berries with Whipped Ricotta

5 minutes

Ricotta and whipped cream are the main ingredients for cannoli filling. Omitting the pastry shell and using less whipped cream, it makes a satisfying and easy everyday dessert. To dress it up, serve with a wafer cookie or biscotti.

- **4 T part-skim ricotta**
- **1 T sugar**
- **2 T whipped cream**
- **$\frac{1}{2}$ t lemon zest**
- **$\frac{2}{3}$ c blueberries**

Wash the blueberries and remove any stems or unripe berries. Mix the ricotta and sugar until the ricotta is loose and fluffy. Fold in the whipped cream and lemon zest. Layer the blueberries and ricotta cream in a wineglass or parfait glass. Desserts do taste better out of a pretty glass. Enjoy!

Variation: Substitute strawberries or raspberries for the blueberries.

Berries should be refrigerated unwashed and washed immediately before eating. Washed berries spoil very quickly. If you wash more than you'll eat, freeze them or toss with a spoonful of sugar and lemon juice.

Spiced Baked Apple

8 minutes

Baked apples are comforting and also delicious. With a sprinkle of granola, or maybe some yogurt, this makes a substantial breakfast as well. One of my kitchen toys is a bowl with a spike for impaling a cored apple, which makes it cook faster. Slicing it in half accomplishes the same thing, without requiring another item competing for shelf space!

1 apple, halved and cored

$\frac{1}{4}$ t cinnamon

1 t butter

1 t sugar, honey, or maple syrup

Optional: 1 T raisins

2 t chopped walnuts

Melt the butter with the cinnamon and sugar in the bottom of a large soup bowl or pasta plate. Pile the walnuts and raisins into two small piles on your dish. Place each apple half face down over a pile of raisins and walnuts, and microwave for four minutes, or until soft.

Rice Pudding

10 minutes

Rice pudding is another dish that can double for a sweet breakfast. With protein, dairy, fruit, and grains all in one dish, you have a good start to the day! I prefer the chewier texture of short grain brown rice or wild rice, but white rice can also be used. Cow's milk, soy milk, or coconut milk can be used with slightly different flavors but equal success.

$\frac{1}{2}$ **c cooked rice**

$\frac{2}{3}$ **c milk**

1 T brown sugar

1 t butter

$\frac{1}{8}$ **t cinnamon**

Dash of cloves

1 egg, beaten

2 T minced dried fruit (raisins, apricots, prunes, etc.)

Optional: 2 T toasted almonds, sliced or chopped

Mix the spices, butter, sugar, milk, and rice in a small saucepan. Bring to simmer. Remove from the heat and gradually beat in the egg. Add the fruit. Return to a burner, and over extremely low heat or in a double boiler, stir until the sauce has thickened. Do NOT allow it to come to a boil. Stir in almonds and enjoy.

Chocolate Covered Cherries

5 minutes

Cherries are a great source of antioxidants, and they taste wonderful with a hint of bitterness from chocolate. Dark sweet cherries are often available in the freezer section of the grocery store.

$^2/_3$ c frozen cherries

1 T dark chocolate chips

Melt chocolate in a small bowl or glass measuring cup, stirring every 15 to 30 seconds. Pour over the cherries, and allow them 3–5 minutes to thaw slightly. Serve plain, or with a garnish of ginger thins or spoonful of vanilla ice cream.

Variation: Substitute $^1/_4$ c dried apricots, soaked in hot water for 20 minutes and drained, for the cherries.

Pears and Cheese

5 minutes

A perfect finish to a hearty winter meal, you'll find that pears are often at their best in the late autumn or early winter. This is my favorite combination, but there are many different combinations you may enjoy.

1 pear

1 oz aged sheep cheese, room temperature

$\frac{1}{2}$ t honey

Black pepper to taste

Slice pear. Slice cheese, and arrange both items on a small plate. Drizzle with honey, and add a light grind of black pepper.

Nutrition Basics

Nutrition is complex on a molecular level, but when it comes to cooking and shopping for food, you can simplify it down to a few basic concepts:

> ➢ Variety
> ➢ Fruits & vegetables

It is helpful to eat whole grains, limit your sugar intake, and avoid drinking too much alcohol. However, focusing on produce and variety are a great start.

Variety

Variety means eating many foods from each food group. While foods within a food group share some nutrients, other nutrients are only available in some foods. Eating a range of items ensures that you get all the building blocks your body needs to function well.

Within each category, you'll find there are foods to eat less often, and foods to eat more often. Variety means eating the "more often" foods daily or weekly and only occasionally eating the "less often" items.

How do I know what is a "less often" food?

An easy guideline is to consider whether your item is a recognizable plant, or if it has been heavily processed. Most animal products should be eaten in small amounts (if consumed at all).

You can also look at the nutrition label. Eat less of foods with:

Trans fat (eat none)

Sugar >10 g

Sat Fat >1.5 g

Sodium > 150 mg

Some healthy foods will have higher values, but you'll be able to recognize them as whole foods, like nuts.

Grains

Grains allowed ancient civilizations to build cities: they are a hardy source of calories that are easily transported and stored. They are primarily carbohydrate, with some protein and a touch of fat. Grains can be broken into two basic categories: refined and whole. Whole grains have all three parts of the grain intact, while refined grains have only the starchy endosperm (the germ and bran have been removed). Whole grains are more nutritious because they still contain valuable nutrients in the bran and the germ—like fiber, iron, and B vitamins. Whole grains are also digested more slowly than refined grains, so they help stabilize blood sugar and hunger.

Reading labels can be tricky. Fortunately, in recent years, whole grains have become more common and labeling is better for whole grains.
But, CAUTION, "multigrain" or "wheat" does not mean whole grain. Read the ingredients to check for oats, whole rye, 100% whole wheat, or whole grain corn meal.

Some examples of whole grains include: oatmeal, 100% whole wheat bread, brown rice, millet, quinoa, whole grain pasta, and whole corn. Refined grains include white bread, pasta, most cakes/cookies, and white rice. When you are shopping, be sure you read the first ingredient on the label of any grain product. For any regularly consumed food, it should always be a whole grain like whole wheat or whole rye. Try to have at least half the grains you eat be whole, but if you are concerned about weight, diabetes, or blood pressure, aim for all whole grains.

Sources of whole grains: whole grain bread, some cereals, oatmeal, popcorn, barley, millet, kasha, quinoa, buckwheat, brown rice, and wild rice.

Serving: 1 slice bread or $^1\!/_2$ c cooked grains.

How many each day? 4–9

Example: 1 small homemade muffin + 2 small slices bread + 1 cup rice = 5 servings

Meat & Beans (Protein)

Protein is essential for repairing and building all your cells. Your body needs many different types of amino acids (the building blocks of protein) to work well. Animal sources of protein, like meat, poultry, eggs, and milk, have all the amino acids you need. Plant sources (except soy) do not. Different plants groups have different types of amino acids, so eating a variety provides all the amino acids needed.

The protein group also tends to be a good source of B vitamins, zinc, and iron. The animal-based proteins can be high in fat—contributing to heart disease and strokes—so choose lean options over fatty options most of the time. Beans are a great source of fiber as well as of protein, iron, folate, and B vitamins. Upset your tummy? Add them gradually to your diet: 2 or 3 tablespoons daily; then add 5 or 6 tablespoons the next week. Try adding them to salad, chili, Mexican dishes, soup, or pasta.

Sources of protein: meat, fish, eggs, nuts, seeds, legumes, dairy, and soy.

Serving: 1 egg, 1 oz cooked fish or meat, 1 T peanut butter, $\frac{1}{4}$ c tofu or cooked beans, 1 oz nuts or seeds.

How many each day? 5–6 servings

Example: $\frac{1}{2}$ cup beans + 3 oz tuna + 1 T peanut butter = 6 servings

What does lean protein mean?

The lean protein category includes foods with less saturated fat, like 93% lean ground beef, dried beans and peas, fish or nuts. Most Americans eat too much meat, and not enough fish and beans for ideal health.

When you cook, you can also make your choices leaner by trimming fat, draining fat, removing poultry skins, not breading, and not frying items.

Dairy

Dairy is a good source of protein and calcium. It also contains helpful nutrients like iodine, potassium, vitamin D, and vitamin A. Look for low-fat options, like 1% or non-fat milk and part-skim cheese. Dairy products often contain high levels of added salt (sodium) and sugars, especially in cheeses and yogurts. Check the labels, and try to choose no added sugar or low sodium options.

Sources of dairy: milk, cheese, yogurt, non-dairy milks. (Choose fortified non-dairy milks. Check the label for added calcium and vitamin D.)

Serving: 1 c or 8 oz milk or yogurt, $1\frac{1}{2}$ oz cheese, $\frac{1}{2}$ c cottage cheese, 8 oz fortified soy or rice milk,.

How many each day? 3 servings

Example: 1 c yogurt + 1 c milk + 2 slices cheese = 3 servings

Fat

Fat is not a food group, but it is an important nutrient. There are many types of fat; basically, we distinguish between trans fats or partially hydrogenated oils, saturated fats, and unsaturated fats. Trans fats literally clog your arteries, so avoid them completely. They are typically found in commercially produced bakery or fried items, but can also be found in spreads such as peanut butter or margarines. Saturated fats are also associated with some heart and brain diseases, and should be limited. Saturated fats are solid at room temperature and mostly found in animal products. Unsaturated fats are generally heart-healthy. Try to eat mostly unsaturated fat found in oils, olives, avocados, seeds, and nuts.

Trans fat is sometimes found on ingredients lists as "partially hydrogenated" oils even when the label says 0 g trans fats if there is less than 0.5 g per serving.

91

Fruits & Vegetables

Both history and research show that fruits and vegetables are the basis of a healthy diet. Every week another article appears touting the benefits of eating one particular berry, type of green, or the skin of apples. It's all true, to some extent, but your best bet is simple: eat a variety of them. Riper fruits and vegetables both taste better and contain more nutrients, so try to shop in season. You can also consider frozen or canned options.

Vegetables

Enjoy your vegetables! They offer a huge range of nutrients, from alpha-linoleic acid and beta-carotene to zeazanthin and zinc. You may be able to buy a multivitamin, but there are beneficial compounds in your vegetables that aren't in your vitamins. The nutrients in vegetables help keep your digestive system running well, your eyes bright, your skin healthy, your immune system kicking, and your red blood cells plump. Eat a variety and you'll go a long way toward keeping your body healthy. And they taste pretty good.

Vegetables are also key in preventing diet-related diseases and unwanted weight gain. Conditions like high blood pressure, heart disease, and diabetes

How do I know when it's ripe?

Experience is the best teacher, unfortunately. Generally, leafy greens should look firm and bright green. Mold, mildew, wilting, or extensive bruising is a sign that it's past its prime.

Look for firm: apples, citrus fruit, summer squash, winter squash, onions, garlic, carrots, potatoes, cranberries, sweet potatoes, grapes, Brussels sprouts, kohlrabi, cabbage.

Look for barely soft: kiwis, avocados, pears, plums, strawberries, tomatoes, peaches, apricots, blueberries.

are very responsive to eating habits. To help prevent cardiovascular disease, cancer, and diabetes; try to fill your plate with half fruits and/or vegetables at each meal. Talk to your doctor or nutritionist about other changes you can make in your life.

Some concrete suggestions for everyone:

➢ aim for green vegetables daily (especially dark leafy greens)

➢ aim for orange vegetables at least five times a week

➢ more color is better: eat red, yellow, white, and purple vegetables too

Vegetables are primarily carbohydrates, with a little bit of protein and fat. They have relatively few calories, except for starchy vegetables such as potatoes and corn, but many important nutrients.

Sources of vegetables: tomatoes, green beans, bell pepper, cucumbers, etc.

Serving: 1 c raw leafy greens, $\frac{1}{2}$ c cooked leafy greens, $\frac{1}{2}$ c raw non-leafy vegetables, $\frac{1}{2}$ c cooked beans.

How many each day? 4–7 servings

Example: 1 c broccoli+ $\frac{1}{2}$ c cucumber + $\frac{1}{2}$ c sweet potato + 1 c baby spinach = 5 servings.

Fruit

There's a reason most kids like fruit. It tastes good, and it is packed with important nutrients such as vitamin C, folate, and fiber. Fiber and water help smooth out your digestive system, while vitamin C keeps your cell membranes solid. Other compounds, like quercertin from apples and reservatol from grapes, can help protect you from heart disease and recover from strenuous exercise.

Eating many colors and flavors offers a range of health benefits. Choosing whole fruit, instead of juice, improves your fiber intake and maximize the nutrients in your servings. Because fruit is also often sold by the piece, you can buy precisely how much you will eat. Just like with vegetables, you want to eat a range of colors because they have different types of antioxidants and beneficial compounds.

Sources of fruit: grapes, apples, berries, melon, raisins, dates, juice, etc.

Serving: $1/2$ small apple, 1 large plum, $1/2$ c fresh fruit, $1/4$ c dried fruit, or $1/2$ c fruit juice

How many each day? 3–4

Example: 1 plum + $1/2$ c berries + $1/4$ c raisins = 3 servings

What's the deal with juice?

Juice, and smoothies made with juice, should be limited. Since the fiber has been removed, your body digests the sugars very quickly. The sugar from the juice enters your blood, and then your body produces insulin to remove it from your blood. The spike and drop can leave you feeling hungry, shaky, or irritable.

Eating food with your juice and limiting serving sizes can help. If you enjoy juice, try to consume it in 4 oz ($1/2$ cup) portions. Plain seltzer can stretch it to 8 oz and add fizz.

What Do I Eat?

Note your fruit and vegetable intake for three to four days. Write the number of servings on the appropriate line, and add to see your total number of servings. Did you eat seven or more?

Item	1 serving	Day 1	Day 2	Day 3	Day 4
Raw leafy vegetables	1 cup				
Raw non-leafy vegetables	$\frac{1}{2}$ cup				
Cooked vegetables	$\frac{1}{2}$ cup				
Small whole fruit	1 per fruit				
Chopped, frozen, or canned fruit	$\frac{1}{2}$ cup				
100% fruit juice	6 oz ($\frac{3}{4}$ cup)				
Dried fruit	$\frac{1}{4}$ cup				
Total servings	--				

Like those numbers? Great, keep up the good work.

Think you could use some change? Keep reading! We'll work on it over the next few pages.

How to Eat More Fruits and Vegetables

First, overcome your own inertia. The hard part of changing eating habits is that they are habits. That can make it incredibly challenging to want to change, much less to actually enact change. One easy step is to simply write down three reasons why you, personally, want to eat more fruits and vegetables:

1._____

2._____

3._____

Great! Feel free to add more reasons or thoughts on a separate sheet of paper.

Next, think about the challenges you face in eating more fruits and vegetables and write them down:

1._____

2._____

3._____

What are some solutions, or ways to approach these challenges? Try to think of two solutions for each challenge, and write them below.

Common Challenges and Approaches

1. **I don't like them.**
    a. Eat the ones you do like—even if you don't like spinach, you probably will eat tomatoes, or carrots, or grapes.
    b. Try new ones, cooked or prepared in different ways.
    c. Practice. Kids take 20 tastes before they like new foods. Adults need to become familiar with new foods slowly too.

2. **They are too expensive.**
    a. Look for less expensive options. Cabbage, for example, is almost always the best deal in the store. Sweet potatoes are often quite affordable.
    b. Compare fresh, frozen, and canned prices to see which is the least expensive that day or week.
    c. Reduce other purchases—can you substitute dried beans or lentils for meat, or frozen orange juice concentrate for juice in a jug?

3. **It takes too much time.**
    a. Check out the recipes in the front of each recipe section. Many take fewer than 15 minutes.
    b. Buy frozen or pre-sliced items—pre-sliced is considerably more expensive, but the time savings might be worth it.

4. **There isn't any healthy food at work.**
    a. Pack your own lunch or snack.
    b. Request healthy options in your cafeteria. They may have dishes you don't know about, or be willing to create a new one.

5. **I don't know how to cook them.**
    a. Try a few recipes. There will be mistakes, probably, but most of your adventures will be good.
    b. Utilize online resources like Epicurious.com to find recipes and instructions.

Incorporating More Produce

Eating more produce starts with buying it. I find it helpful to have an idea, or a vague plan, of recipes when I choose items. Make sure you select items you like and will eat when you grocery shop. Eating more produce doesn't mean you have to eat your childhood horror!

Fresh produce is great, but it can spoil quickly if you buy large packs of different items. Choose items where you can select the volume, and balance your list with items that store well—like carrots and winter squash—and those that do not store well—like spinach and asparagus. Canned or frozen vegetables may be wise choices too. I like to always keep a bag or two of frozen vegetables in the house, whether it is home frozen or commercially frozen.

Try preparing items when you come home from the store to reduce the work you'll need to do later, or set aside time specifically to wash and cut produce for a few days. Having melon or cucumber chunks cut up and ready for snacks or to toss into salads, makes it easy to eat more. Instead of grabbing a cookie, you can reach into the fridge and snag some carrot sticks, grapes, or sliced melon.

Vegetables that I like…

Fruit that I like….

98

Eat Vegetables!

➤ Store produce in the front of the fridge, where you see it.

➤ Measure. Pull out a measuring cup to see how much is actually in ½ cup, or 1 cup. You could be eating more, or less, than you think.

➤ Eat carrot sticks, cucumber slices, pepper strips, fennel slices, celery sticks, broccoli, or cauliflower pieces with hummus or one of the spreads in Spreads, Dips, and Sandwiches for a snack or light lunch.

➤ Start your meals with a salad, vegetable spring rolls on pg. 33, or simple vegetable soup made from broth and diced vegetables.

➤ Nibble on raw vegetables, like cherry or grape tomatoes, and baby carrots, while you cook. It's like salad, but without the lettuce. The fancy name is crudités.

➤ Add extra vegetables to sandwiches: another slice of tomato, sliced cucumber, a handful of spinach, sprouts, onions, etc.

➤ Add extra chopped produce like broccoli, spinach, peas, corn, or carrots to premade meals, like pasta dishes or canned soup.

➤ Eat dried beans or peas instead of meat or poultry for one meal per week or substitute for half the meat in dishes like chili or tacos.

➤ Decrease the pasta and increase the vegetables in pasta dishes.

➤ Try eating vegetables prepared in new ways—raw instead of cooked, roasted instead of steamed, etc.

Eat Fruit!

∗ Store whole fruit in a clear glass bowl, within sight, so you see it.

∗ Pack fruit in your lunch, or for snacks away from home.

∗ Make your own trail mix, with unsweetened dried fruit and nuts.

∗ Add fresh, dried, or frozen fruit to hot or cold cereal.

∗ Eat fruit—bananas and apples are especially good- in peanut butter sandwiches instead of jam.

∗ Use cooked fruit, like Plum Compote on pg. 82, on pancakes and waffles instead of syrup.

∗ Make smoothies, or popsicles from fruit puree.

∗ Eat fruit every day with breakfast, or for dessert. Or both!

Enacting Change

One approach is to take it one step at a time. Select one goal per week, and record it. Make your changes gradually—so if you're eating 2 servings of vegetables per day, try eating 3 per day before trying 4 or 5.

This week, I'll…

_____

_____.

Completed:_____%

This week, I'll…

_____

_____.

Completed:_____%

This week, I'll…

_____

_____.

Completed:_____%

This week, I'll…

_____

_____. Completed:_____%

Challenge Ideas
Try 2 new vegetables.
Eat 3 cups/week of dark leafy greens.
Eat 3 cups/week orange vegetables.
Eat 2 snacks with vegetables.
Eat [3, 4, or 5] servings of vegetables every day.

Eat 3 pieces of fruit.
Try 2 new fruits.
Eat fruit on 3, or 4, or 5 days.
Eat 3 servings of fruit daily.

It takes about three weeks to make a new habit, so congratulations! Creating and continuing challenges can be a great way to work on diet and exercise change. Keep a diary, start a blog, or pair up with a friend if you need extra motivation. Keep up the good work!

Refresher Course

One of the reasons I enjoy cooking and eating is because you both wake up to a new empty plate and mistakes are generally fleeting. Each morning, I have a fresh start. Occasionally, it's helpful to stop and review your choices. Feel free to copy the page below, and check on your habits regularly.

Item	1 serving	Day 1	Day 2	Day 3	Day 4	Day 5	Day 6	Day 7	Day 8	Day 9
Raw leafy vegetables	1 cup									
Raw non-leafy vegetables	1/2 cup									
Cooked vegetables	1/2 cup									
Small whole fruit	1 per fruit									
Chopped, frozen, or canned fruit	1/2 cup									
100% fruit juice	6 oz (3/4 cup)									
Dried fruit	1/4 cup									
Total servings	----------									

Glossary of Food Preparation Terms

Baking – Cooking food in the oven.

Blanching – **Boiling** food briefly but removing it before it cooks through.

Boiling – Cooking food by submerging it in water that is at or above 212°F or 100°C (you should see large bubbles breaking the surface of the water).

Braising – Browning a food over high heat, and then simmering for an extended period (the time depends on the size of the item).

Broiling – Cooking food at a very high temperature with a heat source above the food.

Browning – Cooking quickly over high heat, until the surface of the food turns brown and the inside stays raw.

Caramelizing – Cooking foods slowly until they are browned and are sweeter.

Chopping – Cutting food into pieces of equal size and dimension. Food may be chopped into smaller pieces, such as for a soup, or larger pieces, such as for roasted vegetables.

Coring – Removing the center, typically inedible, part of the food.

Dash – A very small amount of a flavoring, such as a few shakes of pepper.

Dicing – Cutting food into cubes. Typically, the pieces are equal in size and dimension, about ¼ to $^1/_8$ inch across. Large dice are approximately ½"-3/4" in diameter.

Frying – Cooking food by completely submerging it in hot oil.

Julienne – Cutting food into matchsticks.

Kneading – Mixing and pressing the ingredients by hand or in a stand mixer to develop the gluten (for breads) or combine flavors (such as for meatloaf).

Mincing – Cutting food into tiny pieces. Each piece should be about 1/16 of an inch across. This cut is usually used on aromatics such as garlic, ginger, shallots, herbs, or chili peppers.

Mixing – Stirring foods together until they are evenly blended.

Pan Frying – **Frying** food with enough oil to come half-way up the side of each piece of food.

Parboiling – **Blanching.**

Pinch – A very small amount of a seasoning. Slightly more than a **Dash**, it is approximately half of $^1/_8$ teaspoon.

Poaching – Cooking food in a gently heated liquid, generally at a simmer. Usually used for meat, poultry, eggs, fish, or fruit.

Pureeing – Processing cooked or raw foods in a blender or food processor until smooth.

Roasting – **Baking** at a very high heat. Roasting happens in the oven at temperatures of 400°F or more.

Sautéing – Cooking food in a pan with just enough oil or butter to cover the pan's base and prevent it from sticking.

Searing – Cooking food in a pan over high to medium-high heat for a short period of time just to create a flavorful crust on the surface. The fat (if used) in the pan must be very hot, the pan must not be crowded, and no liquid can be added.

Sifting – Putting dry goods, like flour, through a sifter to break up any clumps. Alternatively, the dry blend may be shaken through a fine mesh strainer 2-3 times.

Simmering – Cooking foods in hot water just below a full boil—small bubbles should rise slowly from the bottom of the pot to the surface.

Slicing – Cutting food into thin pieces.

Steaming – Cooking food by holding it in a rack or basket with a lid over boiling water. Less perfect steaming can use a tightly covered pot with ¼" to ½" water in the bottom and food piled in the pot. The very bottom layer will technically be boiled, but the effect is similar.

Stewing – Cooking food slowly in a seasoned liquid, like broth or curry.

Stir-Frying – Cooking food in a pan with just enough oil or butter to cover the pan's base and prevent it from sticking.

Whisking – Stirring briskly with a whisk to beat air into a mixture or to blend it very thoroughly.

Index

Made in the USA
San Bernardino, CA
16 August 2013